Ro

The Film I
written abo
it. Combinin
ysis of tech
many dimen
modern soci

Leo Braudy
University. I
His Films
Hume, Field
A Collection
tieth Centur

FOCUS ON

SHOOT THE PIANO PLAYER

edited by
LEO BRAUDY

A SPECTRUM BOOK

Prentice-Hall, Inc.
Englewood Cliffs, N. J.

Library of Congress Cataloging in Publication Data

Braudy, Leo, comp.
    Focus on Shoot the piano player.

    (Film focus) (A Spectrum book)
    CONTENTS: Braudy, L. Introduction.—Chronology.—
Cukier, D. A. and Gryn, J. A conversation with François
Truffaut. [etc.]
    1. Tirez sur le pianiste (Motion picture) I. Title.
II. Series: Film focus.
PN1997.T53B7   791.43'7   72-8413
ISBN 0-13-809632-5

Illustrations from *Shoot the Piano Player* are reprinted by permission of Janus Films, Inc.

Printed in the United States of America
10   9   8   7   6   5   4   3   2   1

PRENTICE-HALL INTERNATIONAL, INC. (*London*)
PRENTICE-HALL OF AUSTRALIA, PTY. LTD. (*Sydney*)
PRENTICE-HALL OF CANADA, LTD. (*Toronto*)
PRENTICE-HALL OF INDIA PRIVATE LIMITED (*New Delhi*)
PRENTICE-HALL OF JAPAN, INC. (*Tokyo*)

CONTENTS

COMMENTARIES

ACKNOWLEDGMENTS

As always in a project of this kind, many people contributed their time, knowledge, and courtesy. I would like to thank especially Denise Dwyer, Melissa Smith, Amy Hittner, and Tom Leitch, who helped me with the translations; Fred Rubik of Janus Films, who smoothed my way to see the film and the material about it Janus possesses; and Suzanne Schiffman of François Truffaut's office, who kindly gave of her time to answer my questions and hunt up elusive articles.

SHOOT THE PIANO PLAYER

(*Tirez sur le pianiste*)

Films de la Pléiade, 1960

DIRECTOR	François Truffaut
ASSISTANT DIRECTORS	Francis Cognany, Robert Bober, Björn Johansen
PRODUCER	Pierre Braunberger
PRODUCTION SUPERVISOR	Serge Komor
PRODUCTION MANAGER	Roger Fleytoux
PRODUCTION SECRETARY	Luce Deuss
ADAPTATION	François Truffaut and Marcel Moussy from the novel *Down There* by David Goodis (published in France under the title of *Tirez sur le pianiste*).
SCRIPT AND DIALOGUE	François Truffaut
SCRIPT GIRL	Suzanne Schiffman
ENGLISH TITLES	Noelle Gillmor
PHOTOGRAPHY	Raoul Coutard, in Dyaliscope
EDITORS	Claudine Bouché and Cécile Decugis
ART DIRECTION	Jacques Mely
SOUND	Jacques Gallois
MUSIC	Georges Delerue (also plays the piano for Aznavour).[1] Song "Dialogues d'amoureux" composed by Félix Leclerc and sung by Leclerc and Lucienne Vernay; song "Vanille et framboise" composed and sung by Boby Lapointe.

TIME: AMERICAN VERSION, 80 MINUTES; OTHER VERSIONS 84 AND 86 MINUTES

Filmed from December 1, 1959–January 15, 1960 in Paris at a café, Á la bonne franquette, rue Mussard, Levallois and at Le Sappey (about fifteen miles from Grenoble), with an additional two weeks in March 1960 to reshoot several scenes and complete the shooting of others, principally the escape of Charlie and Léna from the attempted kidnapping by Ernest and Momo. First shown in Paris on August 22, 1960; first shown in the United States in New York City on July 24, 1962.

[1] Many of the printed credits for *Shoot the Piano Player* assert that the music was written by Jean Constantin, and one or two of the essays in this volume refer to this. Constantin was in fact asked to do the music and even signed a contract, but never delivered. Georges Delerue was hired in his place.

CAST

Charlie Kohler/Edouard Saroyan	CHARLES AZNAVOUR
Léna	MARIE DUBOIS
Théresa	NICOLE BERGER
Clarisse	MICHÈLE MERCIER
Plyne	SERGE DAVRI
Momo	CLAUDE MANSARD
Fido	RICHARD KANAYAN
Chico	ALBERT RÉMY
Richard	JACQUES ASLANIAN
Ernest	DANIEL BOULANGER
Lars Schmeel	CLAUDE HEYMANN
Passerby who helps Chico	ALEX JOFFÉ
Singer in café	BOBY LAPOINTE
Mammy	CATHERINE LUTZ

Introduction

by LEO BRAUDY

In 1959 Jean Renoir was interviewed during the filming of *Le Déjeuner sur l'herbe*. He spoke wistfully of the contemporary lack of interest in films and wondered aloud whether audiences would ever again attend films as they had in the past. Yet, at almost the same time, in one of the fine coincidences of cultural history, a number of young French film critics, many of them associated with the magazine *Cahiers du Cinéma* and its founder, André Bazin (who considered Renoir one of the great masters in the history of film), were beginning to make their own films. As if in response or in anticipation of Renoir's gloom, directors such as François Truffaut, Jean-Luc Godard, Claude Chabrol, Roger Vadim, Jean-Pierre Melville, Georges Franju, and Alexandre Astruc, often united in little more than their enthusiasm for watching and making films, and their distaste for the "official" French film industry, began a cultural movement that still affects us.[1] If this movement can be described in one word, that word might be "self-consciousness"— at all levels: a self-consciousness about film history and tradition, a self-consciousness about the act of making a film, a self-consciousness in the audience, which approaches a film more as a cultural artifact than as an entertainment for which the mind is turned off, and, perhaps the most important aspect, a self-consciousness about the role of the director, matched with the audience's own increased awareness that the director is a "star" too. Films like Truffaut's *Les Quatre Cent Coups* and Godard's *À Bout de Souffle (Breathless)*

---

[1] Truffaut once remarked that the only thing the so-called *Nouvelle Vague* directors had in common was that they all liked to play pinball machines.

1

accomplished more to change the audience's attitude toward films and their directors than volumes of *Cahiers* articles about *auteur* theory.

The emphasis of this group of directors on improvisation and inexpensive camera methods derived from a pragmatic effort to break away from elaborate French production methods so that young directors could make films without going through long apprenticeship in what they considered to be an aesthetically and personally corrupting system. At one point Truffaut, Godard, and Alain Resnais envisioned setting up an alternate production system; except for *Shoot the Piano Player*, Truffaut has produced all his films through Les Films du Carrosse, his production company, named in honor of Renoir's 1953 film *Le Carrosse d'Or*. Of course, not all the effects of the enthusiasm for film awakened by the *Nouvelle Vague* (as the newspapers called them) were beneficial. Many of these methods heralded an era of "spontaneous" filmmaking that ultimately was to be degraded into the absurdities of handheld camera work in $20 million studio productions solely on the assumption that this was what the public wanted to see. Directors became cultural icons no matter what their real ability, and filmmaking was invaded by the cult of sincerity, by whose canons technical sloppiness automatically spelled deep feeling and technical polish was automatically read as a sellout. Perhaps this confusion of aesthetic values is the price of innovation in films, the art form in which method is most obviously and easily detachable from content—to be imitated insubstantially by whomever has eyes to see. In an article reprinted in this volume, Pauline Kael praises *Shoot the Piano Player* in comparison with "those tiresome well-made movies that no longer mean much to us." [2] A few years later, after a surfeit of films by New Wave epigoni had appeared, she was to long once again for the "well-made" film.

Shoot the Piano Player was a far greater blow to the received assumptions about film method and subject matter than was *The 400 Blows*,[3] Truffaut's first film. Although the improvisations, the

[2] See this volume, p. 78.

[3] I use this familiar translation throughout. In fact, the phrase comes from an expression meaning roughly "paint the town red." Perhaps Truffaut, with his love for American movies, was trying for a French equivalent of *On the Town*.

jump cutting, and the low budget of *The 400 Blows* illustrated many of the new wave innovations in production method, the film still had a story and a situation that was easy to accept, for reasons touched on in some of the essays reprinted in this collection. *Shoot the Piano Player* met more resistance. When it was first released in France the reviews were generally favorable, but the film did mediocre business at the box office because, says Louis Marcorelles, the French public was generally disenchanted with the New Wave. In England and the United States, however, the earlier films of Truffaut, Godard, Resnais, and Chabrol had been drawing large crowds to what were previously small "art" houses. But *Shoot the Piano Player* nevertheless received in England the kind of critical attack described by Gabriel Pearson and Eric Rhode.[4] Perhaps because of the poor British reception, *Piano Player* was not released in the United States until after the great success of *Jules and Jim,* Truffaut's third feature.[5]

Many of the early American reviewers, like Bosley Crowther[6] and Stanley Kauffmann,[7] were struck by what they considered to be the "haphazard" quality of *Piano Player*. Jim O'Connor, reviewing for the *New York Journal-American,* had a typical response. He was offended by what he took to be the film's deliberate meaninglessness, a meaninglessness he equated with highbrow art: "It was aimed undoubtedly to please only the sophisticates. Squares will please go away and get lost . . . Shoot the piano player if you must, but spare foreign film fans from such *chefs d'oeuvres miserables* as this French picture—*s'il vous plaît*." [8] Yet at the same time O'Connor clearly recognizes many important aspects of the film: it's "more like an old-time Mack Sennett comedy movie" and "seemed to be a satire on the American gangster picture." O'Connor is unwilling to believe that an otherwise "sophisticated" French film could also express love of what are to him "unsophisticated" (and therefore obviously well-loved) American comedies and genre films.

---

[4] See this volume, pp. 25–45.
[5] For this reason, several of the essays included in this volume make reference to all three films.
[6] See this volume, pp. 62–64.
[7] See this volume, pp. 60–62.
[8] From a review by Jim O'Connor in the *New York Journal-American,* July 24, 1962.

O'Connor's confusion indicates clearly why *Shoot the Piano Player* deserves critical attention not only for its individual qualities, but also for its importance in the history of taste. Like improvisation, oblique cutting, and low budgets, the aesthetic innovations solidified by *Piano Player* have become part of our unquestioned assumptions about art in general. But it is worth noting the importance of *Shoot the Piano Player* in reeducating us, specifically, to the possibilities of mixed form in art. It is fascinating to note that in 1946 S. I. Bethell could write a book entitled *Shakespeare and the Popular Dramatic Tradition,* in which he instructed his readers, quite rightly, that Shakespeare's audience could react equally well to both the tragic and the comic scenes in a play, for example, like *Macbeth.* We, Bethell implied, could not so react, and the need to recapture the broader aesthetic of the Elizabethan audience was a need to surmount the centuries of criticism that had argued that certain scenes could not have been written by Shakespeare because they "destroyed the tone." It seems strange to cite Bethell's difficulties now because we are so accustomed, on the crudest level, to the mixture of farce and tragedy in films, literature, and even painting. Yet Bethell's efforts ought to be remembered, if only for their present irrelevance. O'Connor still writes at a cultural moment when high art and popular art were two separate and incompatible things. The reeducation of film audiences to the aesthetic possibilities of mixed genre and disruption of tone can almost totally be laid at the door of two works of the early 1960s: Truffaut's *Shoot the Piano Player* and Joseph Heller's *Catch-22.*

I don't want to argue that *Shoot the Piano Player* was unprecedented, even in films. The influence of mixed form in the early sound films of Jean Renoir—such as *La Chienne, Boudu sauvé des eaux,* and *La Nuit du carrefour*—with their sense of the city landscape, requires further study, as does the influence of Roberto Rossellini's experiments with juxtaposed rather than linear narrative in *Paisan,* or his mixture of comic and tragic elements in a sequence like the apartment block search in *Open City. Shoot the Piano Player* is, in fact, preoccupied with tradition instead of being in flight from it. It contains, for example, many references to other films—a usually condemned aspect of New Wave films. But such references at best relate a film to the tradition that produced it (especially relevant for a genre film) and also allude to the pressure of the reality defined by films on our daily lives. In Godard's *Breathless,* this pressure is very specific: Michel, the main character, lives his life in imitation of Humphrey Bogart. The only such characters in *Shoot the Piano Player* are the gun-brandishing gangsters Ernest and Momo. But the film consistently displays a self-consciousness about its past and the process of its making—a few lines of music from Max Ophuls's *Lola Montès,* the appearance of a *Cahiers du Cinéma* delivery truck, the naming of one brother Chico after Chico Marx and Charlie himself after Charlie Chaplin,[9] a remark to the audience about what the censor would do to a nude scene—as an analogy to the preoccupation with the past that is one of the film's main themes. (Until the New Wave directors with their "references" and "homages," films were the least historically-minded of all art forms, without a collective sense of how many of their aesthetic problems had been solved or even formulated.) *Shoot the Piano Player* does not invent the mixture of genres and the disruption of tone—it does reinvent them.

Drawing on his desire to mix genres and disrupt the audience's preconceptions, Truffaut in *Shoot the Piano Player* manipulates those very "disparities" that upset critics such as O'Connor, Crowther, and Kauffmann. Once the gangster plot has been laid down, Truffaut feels free to disregard it and concentrate on what he says really interests him: the characters. He first presents a character that is recognizably stereotyped, and then he gradually humanizes that same character so that the audience's stereotyped reactions are no longer appropriate. In adapting *Shoot the Piano Player* from David Goodis's novel *Down There,* Truffaut makes several changes in Edward Webster Lynn, Goodis's main character: he eliminates

[9] In what may be another tribute to his elusiveness, there is no unanimity about the spelling of Charlie's last name. Various books and articles, the English language subtitles, and Suzanne Schiffman of Truffaut's office all say "Kohler." Other books and articles, as well as a hand-lettered poster outside the café advertising Charlie's act, say "Koller." I have not regularized this in the articles that follow, preferring "Kohler" myself because its obviously Germanic origin looks forward to Jules, the German, and Jim, the Frenchman, and because it implies that the murderous obsession of Julie Kohler in *The Bride Wore Black* may have sisterly affinities with Charlie's detachment.

Lynn's war service so that handling a gun or killing is more alien, and he also eliminates any reference to his ability in a fight.[10] Truffaut's Charlie Kohler is shy; he reads books on how to conquer timidity (perhaps a reminiscence of Renoir's 1928 film *Tire-au-flanc*). Beginning the film with Charles Aznavour fixed in his mind as the lead, Truffaut changes and improvises his own idea of the film in accordance with Aznavour's character. Aznavour has been (and remains) one of the top popular singers in France. His style is personal and melancholic, in which the line between his life and his art is hard to discern, and the dimness of the line one of the main lures for his audience. He either writes his own songs or uses material that similarly projects the image of the *chansonnier,* a type of singer familiar in Europe and akin most closely to Frank Sinatra in the United States. When shooting began on the film, the script had been written until the kidnapping of Fido; much of the rest emerged from the dynamics of the actual shooting.[11]

Although improvisation plays a role in all of Truffaut's films, it is especially important in *Shoot the Piano Player* because the style of the film corresponds to the uncertainties of improvisation, and the themes of the film emphasize the problems of will and improvisation in life, for example, in the contrast between Charlie's hesitations and the voice-over narration that is always telling him how to behave. Even the visual style of the film supports the feeling of improvisation. It illustrates a dual consciousness of both the pressure of fate and the resistance of the characters through their wills; the pressure of the stereotyped plot and the resistance of the "haphazard" scenes (like the first scene with the passerby and the scene with the girl violinist, mentioned so frequently in the essays in this collection); the pressure of mere physical enclosure (in rooms, in cars) and the desire to escape. Truffaut may have removed any mention of Eddie Lynn's physical prowess (cited several times in the novel) because the character of Charlie Kohler, as conceived in the film, is defined more by his head than by his body. Truffaut's attempt to imply a palpable space around his central character, a space that is difficult to penetrate, may be one of his greatest

[10] See this volume, pp. 123–26, for Truffaut's remarks about the adaptation.
[11] For an account of Aznavour's work in the film, see Truffaut's own article in this volume, pp. 95–97.

achievements in adaptation: a physical analogy to Charlie's social and personal isolation in the novel. The entire film is richly available for a discussion of images, settings, and camera movements that enhance this basic relation between freedom and isolation in the definition of Charlie's character: the mirror that reflects his face while he plays the piano, the milk that Fido drops on the gangsters' windshield, the final snow scene at the hideout, where everything is suddenly much too visible—and many more.

The objections that many early critics made to Truffaut's cavalier treatment of the ostensible plot are therefore valid descriptions of what does go on in *Shoot the Piano Player;* but they do not help us to see how Truffaut uses his stereotyped plot to redirect our interest and our imagination toward other themes. We are confused about the reasons why Chico is being chased by Ernest and Momo until it is explained toward the end of the film. But this perfunctory explanation is less important for what it tells us about the plot than for what it reveals of Charlie's personality, especially his background. It strengthens the themes of entrapment and destiny that have been firmly pursued throughout the film. Charlie is afraid of his past, afraid of going back to his family after being a prodigy, afraid of his life as Edouard Saroyan the pianist, content to be uninvolved Charlie Kohler the piano player. The escape that success had promised turned out to be only another trap. It is part of Truffaut's delicacy and his ambiguous handling of the characters that the death of Léna, the waitress who loves Charlie, is much more than a sentimental manipulation of the audience. In fact, Léna represents a threat that Charlie will be returned to the trap of fame; when they first make love, a poster from one of his concert recitals hangs over the bed. She is like the woman who took him away from his brothers to be a famous pianist, and with his return to the piano in the café at the end of the film, there may be a sense of loss, but there is also a sigh of relief. Obviously the theme of the withdrawn and manipulated man who is forced to act, forced to be famous, has great appeal for Truffaut, and one could speculate about the relation of the themes of *Shoot the Piano Player* to his own unexpected success with *The 400 Blows* and his subsequent disillusionments with fame.[12]

[12] See this volume, pp. 119, 153–54.

Truffaut's own difficulties with understanding or at least accept-ing *Shoot the Piano Player* form part of the critical problems still to be resolved about the film and give it an interesting place in his career. In the interviews and comments included in this volume, for example, he both disowns and embraces it on different occasions. What particularly bothers him about the film is what he calls its formlessness, the lack of a central or guiding idea at the start, al-though on another occasion, he commits himself wholeheartedly to the spontaneity and improvisation that the director can bring about on the set and so change the conception of a film.[13] Jean-Paul Comolli has pointed out that Truffaut's method varies between the involved director and the manipulator.[14] One might therefore distinguish between two kinds of Truffaut films, one in which the technique mirrors the story (*Shoot the Piano Player*, or the corre-spondence between "bad boys" and unorthodox methods in *The 400 Blows*), and one in which the technique holds the story at a distance (*Fahrenheit 451* or *L'Enfant Sauvage*). The two possibilities might also be expressed as the tug-of-war between Charlie and his superego in *Shoot the Piano Player*. For all his commitment to mixed genres and the truth of spontaneity in *Shoot the Piano Player*, Truffaut, in other places and in other films, remains uneasy with his own children. Where Jean Renoir controlled sentiment with irony in his films, Truffaut too often resorts to the schizo-phrenic relation between character and off-screen voice. In *Shoot the Piano Player*, in *Jules and Jim*, and most recently in *Les Deux Anglaises et le Continent*, he employs a tone of rapid-fire coldness for the narration of strongly emotional scenes or to make strongly emotional speeches.

The problem for the critic of Truffaut is not the method itself, for it succeeds very well in *Shoot the Piano Player* and *Jules and Jim*. The difficulty lies in the frequent inertness of the relation between the two voices of Truffaut's films, between, one might say, the influences of Jean Renoir and Alfred Hitchcock. Robin Wood, in an excellent article on Truffaut and Chabrol and their relation to Hitchcock, has pointed out that "It is easy to see a connection between the indecisiveness of the Truffaut hero and the need for

[13] See this volume, pp. 13, 123–24, 133–37, 146.
[14] "Au Coeur des paradoxes," *Cahiers du Cinéma,* no. 190 (May 1967): 18.

artistic father-figures evident in Truffaut's own career—the need to identify himself with a fully formed and definite artistic personality." [15] Such a remark also can refer to André Bazin, as well as to Hitchcock and Renoir. But now that Truffaut seems to have come to terms with all three, by publishing his book on Hitchcock and collecting Bazin's articles and notes for a book about Renoir, his own more detached and authoritarian side seems to be getting stronger. At the press conference in New York for the Film Festival showing of *L'Enfant Sauvage,* Truffaut remarked that the theme of the film was the need to discover that one must often hurt someone in order to help them, an intriguing change from his sympathy with the world of the child in *The 400 Blows.*[16] Too many of the problems of method and theme stated by *Shoot the Piano Player* seemed shunted to the side in Truffaut's later films. After the critical failures of *La Peau Douce* and *Fahrenheit 451,* he appears less willing to work ambiguously and risk being misunderstood by his audience. The "beguiling quality" of the later Antoine Doinel films (*Stolen Kisses, Bed and Board*) seems to bespeak a willingness "merely" to entertain, foreshadowed in many of the remarks he makes in this volume about films as spectacle. Instead of complexly presenting the paradoxes of theme and method that make *Shoot the Piano Player* such a classic, Truffaut in his later films may have returned to his piano, safe again from the world.

[15] *Movie,* no. 17 (winter 1969–70), p. 16.
[16] In *L'Enfant Sauvage,* of course, Truffaut himself plays the teacher.

Chronology

1932   Born February 6 in Paris, the only son of Roland Truffaut and Janine de Monferrand; lives with his grandmother until 8; studies at the Lycée Rollin in Paris but spends most of his time playing hooky in movie theaters.

1946   Leaves school and has a succession of odd jobs.

1948   Is caught stealing copper doorknobs to help finance a film club he has founded with a friend; his father has him locked up at the Center for Delinquent Minors at Villejuif. André Bazin helps him to get out of the reformatory, takes him into his home, and gets him a job at Travail et Culture, a cultural lecture group founded by former Resistance members.

1951   After working briefly in a welding shop, joins the Army.

1952   Deserts the Army on the eve of departure for Indochina (after signing up as a three-year volunteer); Bazin persuades him to turn himself in and he spends six months in the Dupleix Barracks prison and the Villemain hospital until he is released for "instability of character" in 1953.

1953   Works for the documentary film department of the French Ministry of Agriculture; is fired; joins the staff of *Cahiers du Cinéma*, recently founded by Bazin; later also becomes a film critic for *Arts*.

1955   Makes short *Une Visite* in 16mm, edited by Alain Resnais.

1956   Research assistant to Roberto Rossellini on three unreleased films.

1957   Makes short *Les Mistons;* becomes noted as a critic for attacking French producers like Ignace Morgenstern, whom he believes are strangling the French film industry; October 29: marries the daughter of Ignace Morgenstern.

1958   Makes short *Une Histoire d'Eau* with Godard; *Les Mistons* shown at Brussels and wins an award; Truffaut is banned from the Cannes Festival for his articles attacking the Festival.

1959   *Les Quatre Cent Coups* wins the Grand Prix at Cannes; Truffaut credited with the script for *À Bout de souffle*, directed by Godard.

1960   *Tirez sur le pianiste;* Truffaut signs "Le Manifeste des 121," an appeal organized by Jean-Paul Sartre of 121 intellectuals asking French soldiers to desert rather than fight in the Algerian War.

1961   *Jules et Jim;* appears as codirector (with Claude de Givray) on *Tire-au-flanc 1962* (a remake of a 1928 Renoir film): through his production company Les Films de Carrosse (after Renoir's *Le Carrosse d'Or*) produces *Tire-au-flanc* and *Paris nous appartient.*

1962   "Antoine et Colette" episode from *L'Amour à vingt ans.*

1964   *La Peau Douce.*

1966   Makes *Fahrenheit 451* in England, his first and so far only film in English; publishes *Le Cinéma selon Alfred Hitchcock,* a lavishly illustrated record of a long interview.

1968   *La Mariée était en noir; Baisers Volés;* Truffaut is involved in organizing strikes to protest the French government's dismissal of Henri Langlois, the head of the Cinémathèque Française (*Baisers Volés* begins with a dedication to Langlois and a shot of the locked doors of the Chaillot Cinémathèque); with Godard helps to close down the Cannes Festival in the wake of the students' and workers' strikes of May 1968.

1969   *La Sirène du Mississippi; Le Domicile Conjugal.*

1970   *L'Enfant Sauvage;* edits and introduces a collection of André Bazin's published and unpublished writings about Jean Renoir.

1971   *Les Deux Anglaises et le Continent.*

A Conversation with
François Truffaut
by DAN A. CUKIER and JO GRYN

Question. Do you see a continuity in your work from *Les Mistons* to *Jules et Jim?* *

Answer. I believe that everything is connected. *Jules et Jim,* which I tend to see as the synthesis of my three films, has several points in common with *Les Mistons:* the importance given to nature, to the rather literary commentary, and to the sensations of the sun. With *Les 400 Coups,* I followed a similar procedure, which consists of showing a character that one disapproves of a priori and then forcing the public to like him. Many of the people who read the scenario had a kind of fear that it would result in something disagreeable. During the shooting, there was the same balancing operation. When you felt that the character was going too much in one direction, you had to direct it towards another, and so, again in common with *Les 400 Coups,* there was a certain "gearing" aspect, beginning from a light, familiar, and simple situation and then tightening the vise mercilessly until one sees that there are no finalities; beginning therefore from gaiety and going towards something stifling. The common point with *Le Pianiste* is my desire no longer to have a division between the sympathetic and the un-

Translated from "Entretien avec François Truffaut," Script 5 (April 1962): 5–15. Copyright © 1962 by Script. Reprinted by permission of Script and Jo Gryn.

* [The following are the English-language translations of the Truffaut titles referred to in this interview: *Jules and Jim (Jules et Jim), The 400 Blows (Les 400 Coups), Shoot the Piano Player (Le Pianiste), Breathless (À bout de souffle), Love at Twenty (L'Amour à vingt ans).*—ED.]

sympathetic characters in a film. That desire came to me in reaction against *Les 400 Coups* where the boy was finally liked too much in compared to his parents.

Q. Le Pianiste is the story of a man alone; *Jules et Jim,* the story of a friendship. That's a striking contrast . . .

A. The idea behind *Le Pianiste* was to make a film without a subject; to express all I wanted to say about glory, success, downfall, failure, women, and love by means of a detective story. It's a grab bag that I have a tendency to disown, although many people prefer it to my other films, because it was a directionless ramble. I believe that the film would have been better if I had had a firmer idea at the outset. With *Jules et Jim* I rediscovered the principle of *Les 400 Coups:* have a strong story at the beginning and it will be strong at the finish, although you must give it a lot of life along the way. I was more at ease filming *Jules et Jim* than *Le Pianiste* because in making *Le Pianiste* I was aware that I had the wrong subject.

Q. What excited you then in Goodis's novel?

A. The style. In *Jules et Jim,* on the other hand, it was both the style and the theme that enchanted me. In Goodis's novel there were things more removed from my own experience; it's a masochistic novel, a little psychoanalytic. Well, I don't like psychoanalysis. Besides, I betrayed it in a certain way because the novel is very pure and the film isn't pure at all; the characters are very different.

Q. What did you add?

A. In *Le Pianiste* there is at times a fidelity to Goodis's tone, but never to his spirit, while in *Jules et Jim* what isn't in the original novel could be. The book is so clear for me, I know it so well by heart, that when I invented something, it was something that would have pleased Roché. So, when Catherine lists French wines or when Jim tells the story of his friend the artilleryman, you can imagine very well that it's in the book.

Q. Why did you speed up the rhythm of Lapointe's song?

A. When I knew him, he sang like that. He sings a little less quickly now because he has become more professional. He's a man with a tremendous timidity who has had a lot of difficulty deciding

to sing. He was dying so of stage fright that he sang at top speed
to overcome it. I liked the rhythm very much because I found it so
jarring!

Q. There is a scene in *Le Pianiste* that we never understood: at
the moment when Aznavour is going to have an audition, and the
young girl leaves. What is she doing in the story?

A. It's actually an unclear scene, but I'm very much attached to
it. I didn't want to show the audition ending because that's a
stereotype of the American cinema. There's a continual parody of
the American cinema in *Le Pianiste,* but there were scenes I refused
to make. Aznavour is going to an audition that's important for
him, and he's going to be successful. I wanted us to stay outside
the door, and at first I thought I would have people strolling in
the corridor and then stop. But the idea of having a lot of people
bothered me, and little by little I found that it would be amusing
to replace a group by a single woman. She plays the violin, stops,
goes out . . . thus opening the door to Aznavour who perhaps
would never have rung the doorbell, who might not have gone in.
This man has passed by this woman. They could have loved one
another, they could have lived together, he a piano player, she a
violinist. It's the meeting of a piano and a violin, of a man and a
woman. The camera stays on this woman; she walks normally, hears
the playing, and stops to listen. Just after you see her in close-up,
you pull back and see her in silhouette in the hall. I wanted this
scene to be spellbinding, and I used a very beautiful woman.

What's amusing is that this scene can be interpreted in many
ways. Those who see the film a second time then say, because now
they know that the impresario is a bastard, that he's made fun of
the girl and that's why she has a sort of disarrayed look. Others
think that she's failed the audition and believes that Charlie is going to succeed.

Actually everything began from the fact that in the scenario
there was an audition I wanted to keep and a girl I wanted to have
act, but who is incapable of speaking dialogue. I used that girl
again in *Jules et Jim*; someone there says about her: "she isn't a
complete idiot, she's hollow . . . she's sex in the pure state . . ."
This scene, slightly outside the plot, is built on the strangeness of

this girl, whom you will certainly see again in my next films because she's become a fetish for me.

Q. It's said that *Les 400 Coups* is an autobiographical film. Does that remain true for the characters of *Jules et Jim*?

A. Jules et Jim is farther from me than the other two films, but the book is completely autobiographical. Let's say that for me it was not *autobiographical,* but *biographical.* Fundamentally I am especially interested in real experiences. That's why I wouldn't like to make a suspense story or a very ingeniously constructed story. I very much enjoy feeling the life in a book or in an original scenario and trying to breathe into it the maximum oxygen while filming. Moreover, I need a struggle; if the scenario had been "won" in advance, it wouldn't have interested me. I need to have a bet to win. It's important for me that the film not be the same at the finish as it was at the beginning.

Q. Le Pianiste has a more aggressive tone than *Jules et Jim,* a film that's more perfect, more "classic." What's the reason for that?

A. In *Les 400 Coups* the subject was so important that the film passed slightly into the background; I had so many scruples that I filmed humbly, as if it were a documentary. I wanted to make some formal discoveries, a desire I satisfied with *Le Pianiste. Jules et Jim* is in that measure the synthesis of the other films; it's simultaneously a great subject that sweeps you away—one you never regret having chosen throughout the filmmaking—and it's a creative venture that inspires ideas that are at the same time formal and moral, visual and intellectual. Everything works together; that's why it's exciting.

Q. You transformed certain newsreels into big screen and left others in standard size. Why is that?

A. There's a very precise reason. You can't transform into scope documents that were filmed in standard. But when I realized that they were nicer in scope, I edited so that the sequence ended with shots that had no people in them. These are the blown-up shots that don't suffer distortion. In fact they weren't modified in the laboratory; they were left as they were. It's clearly a more beautiful effect: all of a sudden the war becomes openly more monstrous— a logical thing to happen.

Q. What led you to use two unknown actors?

A. At first the idea that it was provocative, in certain films, to build confrontations between stars. The public believes in the story, it's going to see a match, it's going to see if Michèle Morgan will be stronger than Bourvil. I'm a believer in surrounding a star with new faces. The shock will be stronger. Opposite Jeanne Moreau I put Oskar Werner because I had been thinking of him since *Lola Montès.* I knew he would be absolutely ideal to play Jules. For Jim, I looked in Paris for a young man for a long time. I saw Serre in minor stage roles; I ran some tests with him, and I was happy.

Q. Weren't you afraid that Jeanne Moreau would overwhelm her partners?

A. No, the role was perfect for her. Among the women who have a name in the cinema she was the only one ·able to play a role which required so much authority and humility at the same time. Since it was a ticklish business, bordering on bad taste, it was necessary to choose a very intelligent actress to get certain things across. If the film isn't spoiled, I believe it's often because of her. There are scenes which, acted by someone else, would have encouraged laughter. There are, in effect, things which must be said with force so as to intimidate the audience in the theater. In a film, as soon as you talk about physical love, the public suddenly becomes very infantile, like a child at an awkward age, and you have to take account of this. One knows very well that such a cue risks laughter. Therefore the next retort must come very quickly. Likewise, certain things produce laughter if the characters say them in bed, for example; and if the commentary becomes delicate, I pass quickly to an exterior shot, the chalet shown by a traveling shot in a helicopter, so that the beauty of the countryside locks the laughter in people's throats. On the whole, according to the public showings I have seen, I wasn't so wrong. This game of risk amuses me very much. I sense that people are completely irritated for a moment: they are going to hate the film; and they are won back by the next scene . . . except for a few who tune out completely for the last twenty minutes, in particular when Catherine meets Albert again (the pajama scene).

Q. You told Marcorelles that *À bout de souffle* was the only film of the New Wave to have been a success. And you also said one day that the films of the New Wave were personal films, addressing themselves only to a special audience. Therefore, it seems natural to us that these films don't attract many people and have only a limited success.

A. There is a kind of democratic equality in the cinema; it depends on the way you see things. You can make films while saying to yourself: "I am warning people in advance about what they're going to see; only those interested in the subject are going to come." Myself, I don't believe in that. I know very well that today people more and more go to see a film rather than just go to the movies. Nevertheless I hold onto the idea that someone can enter the theater by chance, and I know that in a big city five people out of ten come in in the middle of the film. You have to remember that. I am bent on making films that have the same value for everyone in the theater, for those who come in without even looking at the title, for those who read all the reviews, for those who read the book . . . If I had ideas about films that didn't fit that framework, I would film them in 16 mm or I would make them for television . . . I hold onto the idea of an anonymous cinema, an entertainment. It's not a question of making concessions, nor of telling oneself "that's too strong for them, I'm not going to direct it." It's a question of doing what one wants to do, but of always thinking about the way to improve it. I see that as a supplementary discipline. In those interviews that you allude to, I said precisely that since *À bout de souffle,* no *first* film has been a success. I don't consider *Jules et Jim* to be a New Wave film because it's my third film and it cost much more than the others. It's a normal film. The success of *Marienbad,* of *Jules et Jim,* and, in a few weeks, of *Cartouche* (if *Cartouche* is a success) could help my friends, especially since last year was so disastrous in France on the commercial level. When a film by a dedicated director falls on its face, they say: "his film fell on its face"; when it's one of our films, they say: "the young are screwed up, the New Wave is finished." Each time the whole lot of us are put in question!

Q. The claims and arguments that you made as a critic, do you make them as much as a director?

A. I am no longer a theoretician; I am interested in films with less passion, more detachment, a lot of curiosity, but also more indulgence. I can love a film for ten minutes, which was impossible before. I apply *la politique des auteurs* much less; the idea that a good director can ruin a film occurs to me much more. But I retain a great curiosity about the cinema; from time to time, when a film excites me, I get tremendously enthusiastic, but I no longer want to reform the French cinema, or the European, or the world. As far as what I wrote in *Cahiers* is concerned, I believe that everything I said was necessary to do and wished for, has been done.

Q. Who are your masters?

A. Renoir, for everything. He is the proof that everything can be done in the movies with the condition that things be approached with honesty and simplicity. It's said that he's a homey filmmaker, but he has also made some very lyrical and delirious things that he made a success thanks to his spirit of simplicity and humility. I know all of Renoir's films by heart and I always guess how and why he did things. When I have difficulties in my films, I resolve them by thinking of him. It's happened very often that I helped actors to find the right tone for a difficult scene by thinking of the way Renoir would have played it.

Q. And among the Americans?

A. In particular there is Hitchcock. For all the problems of the camera, for the things that have to be expressed in the cutting by a succession of shots, when there is a fleeting moment when it is necessary to cut into ten shots, there he is unbeatable. It's in scenes of this type that lack of craftsmanship is paralyzing. When the staging must be efficient, I believe it's necessary to think of Hitchcock rather than Renoir. Besides he is the only one I see a film by every week. He's a genius.

I can't give you an example of where that helped me in *Jules et Jim,* but in *Le Pianiste* there are things done in that spirit. So, when the kid throws the milk bomb on the car, and we see Aznavour after the wiper clears the milk off the windshield, that's a completely Hitchcockian idea. I never would have managed in *Les 400 Coups* if I hadn't thought of Hitchcock in the scene when the mother comes to find her boy in class. It was very hard to do because

I didn't know whether I should first show the mother, the window, the school principal, the teacher, or the boy. It was while reflecting and completely analyzing the scene that I found the way. The whole succession of shots is done with glances. There's the teacher who notices something behind the glass door, then again the teacher who goes to join the principal. At this moment there is a medium shot of Jean-Pierre, who is a little upset and believes the talk is about him; then a silent intrigue between the principal and the teacher; a close-up shot of Jean-Pierre and his friends, who begin to suspect something when they see him grow pale. Then a shot that didn't work in the centering, but very Hitchcockian in idea—the principal's finger beckoning the child. It's an entirely diabolical trick, followed by the child pointing to his chest—"who, me?"—and finally the arrival of the mother behind the pane, with an unrealistic glance in the classroom. There's where the talent of Hitchcock lies: guessing the moment when it's no longer necessary to be realistic. Logically, a mother who arrives in a class doesn't know where her son is, so her glance must survey the class. But if her glance wanders, it's not efficient, and it was for that reason that I made her look directly at the boy, as if she knew where his seat was in class. Thus, the look petrifies because it looks at us, it looks at the camera. I've often verified the efficacy of this scene in movie houses, and I've heard people scream. That's the only scene that had to be made that way. If it succeeded, I thank Hitchcock, to whom I owe the cutting. That doesn't mean one has to imitate all the time. Thus, the preceding scene, when the boy says his mother is dead, is very personal. I knew intimately how to have it played, and I was sure not to make a mistake. The boy's friend had told him," since you don't have an excuse note, you've got to think up something catastrophic." That's all the kid knows when he comes up. Someone might think that he had foreseen his lie, that he might be going to collapse—that's the idea of the scene. Then his teacher says to him, "show me your excuse note." The boy replies, "I haven't got a note"; the teacher then gets very violent: "you haven't got a note . . . that won't do at all," and the boy tries to summon up his enormous lie, and maybe he won't dare say it. "—It's my mother, sir, my mother . . ." and there, to provoke the lie, the teacher must be very odious: "—Your mother,

your mother, what's with your mother, anyway?" And it's because
he provokes him that the boy has the courage to take the plunge:
"Well, she's dead," while looking him straight in the face. In the
course of my three films I don't believe I've ever directed anyone
with as much precision as Jean-Pierre Léaud in this scene because
I knew exactly what I wanted. I even told him to think "That
annoys the shit out of me" while speaking and to keep that in
mind. It often helps an actor if you tell him what to think just
before or just after a line. This lie he tells is so enormous that the
only way to say it is to be forced by events. After the mother behind
the pane and the father's slap, we again see the boy, who has decided not to return home. At this point there's some rather difficult
dialogue because it's a little unrealistic for a child's speech; but
it must not make people laugh. It's the moment when the boy
says, "After that slap, I can no longer return home; I'm going to
disappear; I'm going to live my life." That's an excessive trick.
You have to think of the mentality of a child to understand something like this because, for a child, everything is out of proportion.
It's just as hard to act; acted emphatically, it would be ridiculous.
I managed it by thinking of Renoir because it's a problem of acting
and not of technique.

I thought about that scene in *La Bête Humaine* when, early in
the morning, Gabin, after having killed Simone Simon, comes to
work and stands next to his locomotive. Then he says to Carette,
with total forlornness and an extraordinary simplicity: "Well, look,
I'll never see her any more. I've killed her, you know . . . we'll
have to keep working . . ." What's wonderful here is to have said
so simply something so out of the ordinary. At that moment in my
film, I made Jean-Pierre play like Gabin to help him find his expression.

These influences are invisible, underground; they are the real
thing influencing the work. But no one would think of *La Bête
Humaine* while seeing that scene in *Les 400 Coups*.

Q. Is it absolutely impossible to feel the influences?

A. A diabolical fellow, like Rivette, is strong enough for that.
You could find technical influences, like Hitchcock's. But no one
would think that there was anything Hitchcockian in *Les 400*

Coups. The critics note the exterior resemblances, the subject, the theme, the decor, the situation, but not the really profound influences.

Q. Is it true that you have rejected *Les Mistons?*

A. That depends on my state of mind. Some days I feel contrary; if someone says something bad about it, I feel like defending it. Other times, I totally agree. Objectively I find that it's really necessary to go back to my original intentions in order to like *Les Mistons.* The execution leaves a lot to be desired; the actors and the dialogue are horrible; the whole thing is enormously crude and gauche. Maybe one can see what I wanted to do and that's why people have been indulgent. I feel like pulling it out of circulation when I see it. There are, nevertheless, some nice things in it, like Bernadette Lafont and the feeling of the sun. But I believe one needs a lot of indulgence to love it. If I had to do *Les Mistons* over again, it would be a lot better. The shots would follow each other normally.

Q. What are your plans for the future?

A. I've just made a half-hour sketch with Jean-Pierre Léaud. It's the French sketch of an international film. Wadja just finished the Polish part, the Italian sketch was done by Renzo Rossellini, the German by Marcel Ophuls, and a young novelist is making the Japanese sketch. The film is called *L'Amour à vingt ans,* and my sketch is a sequel to *Les 400 Coups,* the first sentimental adventure of the same character, whom we see again at seventeen. Besides that, I'm thinking of doing a theatrical production. I've developed a taste for the theater now, but I used to detest it. In films one works too fast; one is too preoccupied with technique; one tends to hamper the actors' work a little. I thought that it would be interesting to concern myself only with the actors. But I still have to find a play.

I Wanted to Treat
SHOOT THE PIANO PLAYER
Like a Tale by Perrault:
An Interview with François Truffaut
by YVONNE BABY

"My critical tendency leads me to work always 'in reaction against.' Thus, *Shoot the Piano Player* is in reaction against the primitive detective film in which the overemphasis on violence attempts to make up for the lack of talent. I also react against the humanized *film noir* in which the gangsters look at each other with watery eyes and the honest people act like scum. That's why I showed gangsters who were simultaneously grotesque and sympathetic, but stripped of sentimentality. Instead, there are no privileged persons in the entire *Piano Player;* you must love them all equally.

"Because spectators see the same scenario in so many films, they have become good scenarists and can always foretell what's coming and how it's going to end. With *Piano Player* I would like them to go from surprise to surprise.

"I also wanted to react against the brutality of the idea of the invulnerable 'tough guy.' Charles Aznavour—whom I wanted to hire since I saw Georges Franju's *La Tête contre les murs*—is vulnerable, and in spite of his timidity, women are attracted to him."

—What's the real theme of the film?

"The love and relations between men and women. Around this story of a piano player who once had been a success, but who chose anonymity after a personal tragedy and now plays an old honkytonk piano, there is a unity in the theme of love.

"The visual action of the film is strictly detective story. So the dialogue never concerns itself with the action but with the relations between men and women in all their modes: sentimental, conjugal, carnal . . ."

—How have you treated the subject?

"I systematically practiced a mélange of genres and sometimes I didn't hesitate to parody. For example, the scene in which Nicole Berger throws herself out of the window is a melodramatic and respectful parody of certain American films. In this way I pay homage to the works of Nicholas Ray and Samuel Fuller, to name only two, and more generally to American B-movies.

"I wanted—it's a structural idea—to delimit the subject in the manner of a tale by Perrault. I had already been struck by the tone of Goodis's novel which, at a certain point, passes beyond the usual gangster novel to become a fairy tale. *Piano Player* isn't made to be believed, but to divert, to amuse."

—Do you pay attention to public reaction?

"For me the cinema is a show, and I compare a film to an act in the circus, or in a music hall, where for once death spoils the entertainment. There are two kinds of writers: those who think about the public and those who don't. For the first kind, of whom I'm one, a commercial failure is a failure of the whole film. I agree with Hitchcock on this point: when one of his films flops, he says, 'I made a mistake.' That means that *Piano Player* is a work for people who love movies; that means it isn't meant for those who go to the movies only once a year."

—Why did you hire an unknown for the principal feminine role?

"The French cinema has at its command a parcel of young actresses less than thirty years old who seem to me to have a dismaying lack of authenticity. These Mylenes, Pascales, Danys, Pierrettes, and Danicks are neither 'real' young girls nor 'real' women, but 'sex kittens,' 'dames,' or 'pinups.' You have the feeling they were created by the movies and for the movies, and they wouldn't exist if the movies didn't. They appear for a year, sometimes two, and then vanish the way they came. For three seasons the distributors and the producers make you use them in films as if they were stars, when in fact they haven't made one viewer come to the film, and nine times out of ten their personal sophistication threatens the verisimilitude of the role they've been given. That's why I wanted to use an unknown for the principal role in my film. Marie Dubois (her pseudonym is the title of a novel by Jacques Audiberti) is neither a 'dame' nor a 'sex kitten'; she is neither 'lively' nor 'saucy.' But she's a perfectly worthy young girl with whom it's conceivable you could fall in love and be loved in return. You wouldn't turn around to look at her on the street, but she's fresh and gracious, a little bit of a tomboy and very childlike. She is violent and passionate, modest and tender."

—Does *Shoot the Piano Player* have anything in common with *The 400 Blows?*

"Yes, in the sense that both films follow a character from one end to the other of a story and draw his portrait. In *The 400 Blows* it was Jean-Pierre Léaud, here it's Aznavour. Talking about childhood carries a terrible responsibility and makes you more conscientious. That's no doubt why it was much easier to direct *Piano Player* after *The 400 Blows*. I had no qualms about the subject. I wasn't afraid of bad taste or excess. I felt more detached, more gay, more relaxed. There isn't any scene in the film that wasn't made for pleasure."

—Is the film more comic than tragic?

"It's both. With *Piano Player* I wanted to make women cry and men laugh."

Cinema of Appearance
by GABRIEL PEARSON and ERIC RHODE

Without doubt, the best films of the New Wave have been associated with a radical change in filmmaking. Though their innovations are often startling, we should not be blinded by this from seeing them as part of a more general revolution in which our idea of art, or consciousness itself, may have been subtly transformed.

PART ONE: THE HUMANIST'S APPROACH

As humanists, our first reaction to the most extreme examples of this revolution—Godard's *Breathless* and Truffaut's *Shoot the Pianist**—is as much one of bewilderment as of pleasure; for these films, according to our theories, shouldn't work. They break most of the rules of construction; sequences are barely connected; moods veer violently and without explanation. Like a cat teasing a ball of wool, the thread of a tale may be arbitrarily picked up, played with, and just as suddenly dropped. As for morality (if there is a morality), we are given few indications of how we should understand its alien logic: characters apparently behave without motive, their feelings remain unpredictable. Moreover, we feel that this is a contingent art, created on every level by improvisation—a procedure which affronts our belief in the artifact as a contrived and

From Sight and Sound *30, no. 4 (Autumn 1961): 160–68. Reprinted by permission of Gabriel Pearson, Eric Rhode, and* Sight and Sound.

* [This is the title of the film as it was released in England—ED.]

calculated work. It is as though, having landed on the moon, we were confronted by a lunar art.

For our intensity of response confirms these films as works of art. And here we notice the first of two contradictions. Although apparently outraging every principle of organization, they are not chaotic. On the contrary, they cohere beautifully. And second, though their very being is improvised, they move with a deftness and aplomb that is almost scornful.

The aim of this investigation is to explore these contradictions and try to resolve them, if only partially. This undertaking would be pedantic if it were restricted to *Breathless* and *Shoot the Pianist,* both of them relatively slight films. What interests us is that these two contradictions, expressed here in their most extreme form, are found to varying degrees in the most recent films of Antonioni, Resnais, Bresson, and Wajda; in such plays as *The Connection* and *Waiting for Godot*; and, moving out into another field in certain types of nonfigurative painting. To investigate the New Wave, therefore, may throw back an unusual light on what at first seem a number of widely disparate works of art.

The critic must have some basis of understanding with a film before he can analyse it. Otherwise his comments, however intelligent, will be continually off the mark. As in politics, there must be a common language before negotiations can take place.

Jacques Siclier's article on New Wave and French cinema in the Summer number of *Sight and Sound* is a case in point. We have here an intelligent humanist who is unable to come to terms with the new movement. Lacking the vocabulary by which he can both define his response to these films and at the same time make evaluations from a humanist standpoint, his argument, though for the most part logical, remains at one remove from the subject. We see this most obviously in his conclusion: "Progressively this young cinema is losing itself behind a curtain of smoke and dreams; and this cinema, which has been described as representative of its time, is in reality as remote from the actual as anything one can imagine."

In using such phrases as "losing itself behind a curtain of smoke and dreams" and "remote from the actual," Siclier is taking certain assumptions for granted. But this makes his position extremely vulnerable, since it is on just these points that apologists for the New Wave would challenge him. Their argument would be that the humanist approach, though admirably decent, provides us with an unsatisfactory approach to criticism since it presupposes a stable reality (implied in such terms as "actual") which we can no longer believe in. For many reasons, they would continue, reality has become as arbitrary as smoke and dreams. There is no curtain, and there is no "actual" as Siclier would have it.

Faced by this challenge, the humanist critic may at first feel—as perhaps Siclier doesn't—that his position is so inadequate that he must abandon it. If he is more tenacious, however, he may hope to discover a vocabulary to resolve the deadlock between himself and the New Wave without a forced surrender of his position. Before he can achieve this, and in order to discover such a basis of understanding, he would first have to analyze his own assumptions. For the sake of clarity, we are summarizing these in note form.

Assumptions of the Humanist Critic

1. Great art is created out of certain conditions, and these conditions are limited. They are:

(a) That in this art both the inner world of the individual and the outer world in all its totality are stable and continuous; that their relationship is dynamic; and that man is equipped, by his reason and imagination, to understand both this world and himself.

(b) That this inner and outer world remain, despite disruptions, in harmony with each other.

(c) That, most important of all, the greatness of this art depends on the extent to which it illuminates the central human predicaments. This concept of centrality is a difficult one to define; for centrality in art, the critic usually points to such literary models as *The Odyssey* or *Anna Karenina*, or to such films as *The Childhood of Maxim Gorki* and *The World of Apu*.

(d) Finally, that this art matches up, however inadequately, to our sense of continuity in the real world. It achieves this by aspiring towards both maximum inclusiveness and maximum coherence. This is brought about by making connections. (See E. M. Forster's "Only connect.")

2. This stable yet dynamic relationship between inner and outer world can best be conceived of in dramatic terms (i.e., dialectically). Because of this a certain type of plot is most useful, a type of plot which develops from:

(a) *Antagonisms*: the most valuable of these play the stable world against some disruptive force, i.e., order against chaos, moderation against excess.
> Ulysses':
> *"Untune that string,*
> *And, hark, what discord follows!"*
describes the most serious development of that conflict.

Fortunately, such discord is usually followed by:
(b) A *dénouement* and *resolution,* in which the world returns to its natural harmony.

3. Having consented to this model of reality, we are then forced to accept further steps in the argument.

(a) The artist holds this balance between inner and outer world at his peril, for if he cannot sustain it in his work his vision of reality is impelled to become *either* a riotous, all-embracing fantasy in which his mind is the controlling authority *or* a "scientific" construction of mechanistic laws in which men are seen as no more than biological automata (cf. Naturalism).
(b) Though these two deviations move in opposing directions, they do, when taken to an extreme, merge into each other and unify; for any aspect of reality becomes indistinguishably grotesque and arbitrary when taken out of total context.[1]

---

[1] The reason for this is complicated. If we sever the connection between an object and its environment, we disrupt the harmony by which parts express wholes. A foot, severed for demonstration, remains significant within a physiological context. But lacking both this context and the body it expresses, the severed foot becomes thoroughly enigmatic and even sinister, as in W. F. Harvey's horror story in which a severed hand scuttles after its victims like a spider and strangles them. Perhaps such inexpressive objects become sinister because they

The misunderstanding between humanist critic and New Wave apologist begins to make itself clear. It arises, as misunderstandings often do, over a confusion of categories. The deadlock in fact is less over an aesthetic than over the theory of reality on which it depends.

In realizing this, the humanist critic finds himself in an impossible position. If he is honest he will accept his opponent's point: that at our present state of knowledge we can no longer believe in a stable reality, since such a belief supposes a hierarchy of values based on a public morality—and none such now holds. This concession breaks the back of his argument. Without a centrality there can be no "arbitrary and grotesque." Therefore the humanist has no reason to describe the New Wave films as failures: he must indeed accept them on their own terms.

This is the situation—stated too drastically, perhaps. Most humanist critics would probably go as far as admitting that they desired, rather than believed in, a stable reality, and that they willingly suspended disbelief as they went about their work. Unfortunately this scepticism does not extend to their critical language. If it did, we would be spared such presumptuous judgments as the *Sight and Sound* reviewer's faulting of *Pickpocket* because it didn't make "the necessary connections," or the BBC critic's rejection of *Breathless* ("The best one can say of it is that it stinks") because its plot lacked conflict. Such comments reveal a failure to recognize how far these films have broken from their humanist prototypes in the nineteenth-century novel and play.

It is over this "how far" that confusion has arisen. If the break had been complete from the start, the inadequacy of the humanist's

---

provide a handy focus for phobias. By contrast, in *The Brothers Karamazov,* Grushenka's foot is for Dimitri almost overexpressive of her sensuality, becoming in fact a fetish.

The Mona Lisa was, for the nineteenth century, the supreme enigma. This was due less to the ambiguity of her famous smile than to her isolation from any usual context, amongst the rocks. Consequently, rather like the severed foot —though reinforced by mysterious feelings about the eternal feminine—she acted as focus for all and every feeling. Pater remarks that "Lady Lisa might stand as . . . the symbol of the modern idea." And indeed it looks as though this still holds. Could not the last shot of Jean Seberg's face in *Breathless* be its contemporary equivalent?

vocabulary would have been obvious. The shift to a completely new kind of film has, however, been a gradual one; and the directors themselves seem to have been barely conscious of it. It is only now, with our complacency disturbed by the New Wave, that we can look back and see the process by which the meaning of such concepts as plot and action has been developed. One can usefully trace such a development from *Bicycle Thieves*,* through *L'Avventura* to *Breathless*.

Bicycle Thieves is apparently conceived in terms of the nineteenth-century theater. The plot exposes a typical conflict: a lone man pitted against the injustices of society. As in a Feydeau farce, De Sica uses objects to further the intrigue—the stolen bicycle is no more than an honorable equivalent of the stolen letter or double bed. Yet by the standards of the well-made play this plot is weak; for the intrigue is undermined by a current of aimless and seemingly irrelevant lyricism. The social conflict in fact is not the plot: it is no more than a theme. The true plot, miming the wayward drift of father and son lost in a labyrinth of streets and piazzas, is the futile search for the illusive thief. This search poses strange, unanswered questions. "What do we mean by a thief, and how can we apply moral categories when we know the situation which makes him as he is?" There is an equally strange transference of guilt, by which the father-as-detective becomes the father-as-criminal. Such preoccupations, though never acknowledged fully, disrupt the plot's manifest action.

Yet it is still rewarding to approach *Bicycle Thieves* in terms of the humanist's idea of plot. This is not so with *L'Avventura,* in which such a plot is both a lure and an irrelevance. Critics have understandably been disturbed by the unexplained disappearance of Anna. As a device this can be justified: it enacts Antonioni's sense of the arbitrariness of experience—the unpredictable workings of memory and feeling. Yet in the last resort the device leaves us uneasy, since the conventions of the film do not prepare us for it. Although Antonioni has moved a long way from De Sica in his discovery of new techniques, he has not come to terms with their

---

* [Released in the United States as *The Bicycle Thief*—Ed.]

similar problem. His plot, too, does not conduct the film's true meaning.

Claudia, the critical and moral intelligence of the film, involves herself with a corrupt society and helps to define it, in much the same way that James's bright young things from America define the corruption of Europe. Yet Claudia, for many reasons, lacks their moral stability; hence the idea of corruption, as exemplified by Sandro and his circle, needs drastic qualification. The conflict is so blurred that moral judgment at first sight becomes impossible. To make sense of *L'Avventura,* in fact, one must initially discard this concept of corruption, with all its satisfying imprecision, in favor of the more neutral concept of failure. For it is surely part of Antonioni's intention, by doing as much justice as he can to the complexities of human relationships, to neutralize such self-approving moral categories.

But first, if only as a form of puzzle about technique, *L'Avventura* helps us to start asking the right questions. What are we to make of Antonioni's camerawork? Those beautiful dolly and tracking shots cannot be understood in terms of the narrative devices of the nineteenth-century novel, upon which so much previous camerawork has implicitly relied. Antonioni's tracking shots do not fulfill any obvious narrative requirement. Yet our aesthetic sense warns us that this ballet of movement is as much part of the film's meaning as the device of Anna's enigmatic disappearance. The difficulty here lies in relating our sense of the "rightness" of these techniques to our general moral sense of what the film is about.

In *Breathless* this difficulty is at its most extreme, and for this very reason it should begin to point the way to a solution. Here there is no gradual shift of conventions to help us to readjust. We are launched immediately into anarchy. We have no apparent choice between blind acceptance and blind rejection. We cannot, as we could with *L'Avventura* and *Bicycle Thieves,* simply go on trying to read the film in our own terms. Here connections are difficult, almost impossible to discover: the camerawork, the editing and the behavior of the characters appear alike random and unmotivated.

Yet the tensions between apparent plot and what actually happens on the screen are not so different from those of its two predecessors. The plot could best be described like this: Patricia is a Jamesian Daisy Miller involved with what one might quaintly call a corrupt young European, Michel. Here, however, the notion of corruption is not even questioned: it is rendered absurd and irrelevant. Michel's banditry and search for a mysterious colleague who owes him money by no means defines what Michel is. On the contrary, the whole notion of corruption is burlesqued, until it ceases to be in any way what the film is about. Hence the apparent plot, of which we could give a clear account in the conventional terms of the hounded thief, is utterly extraneous to the film's action. It becomes indeed what Godard would call *un gag*.

With so little connection between action and plot, all other connections begin to fail us. The usual let-out is symbolism; but here there is nothing like such a meaning. Indeed, as soon as we seize on some aspect of the film as containing symbolic significance, we are immediately contradicted by the action. To be symbolically satisfying, Antonio (the man with the money for whom Michel is searching) ought never to turn up. Yet, aping the conventions of the B-thriller, up he duly pops with the money in the last reel, although he is too late. This too late evokes no irony, however. That sort of moral is not the subject of the film.

And so our confusion increases. Significance is like a chair continually being pulled from under us. We fall with an absurd bump, victims of *le gag*. The more we probe these films, the more enigmatic they appear. The more we try to penetrate their depths, the more we find ourselves involved in a series of shifting, ambiguous surfaces. We are like Alice, trying to walk away from the Wonderland cottage.

PART TWO: THE ARTIST'S APPROACH

The principal reason why the humanist critic has failed to realize the inadequacy of his vocabulary is that the artist himself has been barely conscious of a change in outlook. While ostensibly holding on to the humanist's belief in a stable reality, he has in fact been groping towards an expression which requires a quite different metaphysic.

Pirandello's plays give us a lead. We have here a writer whose artistic insights are ahead of a metaphysic to clarify them. Hence our impression of hesitancy in a playwright who employs many of the modern devices of improvisation. He is hesitant because, despite the utmost scepticism about the notion of centrality, he remains a humanist. Centrality however illusory, exists for him, though he doubts our ability to recognize it. In his *Henry IV* he is still asking whether the madman is sane or the sane man mad, whether the twelfth century is eternally present or irredeemably past. The most challenging question for a humanist—as to whether a central reality exists or not, or whether there is only illusion and therefore an art which can only be illusion imitating illusion—remains unasked.

Six Characters in Search of an Author takes us a stage further. One notices here the title's pun: "author" is both desired author in the ordinary sense and "auctoritas"—a coherent metaphysic which can establish hierarchies among the characters' modes of being and so evaluate and dignify their actions. Their terrible predicament, their anguished states of mind, are both heightened and nullified by the ironic framework within which Pirandello sets them. They are no longer figures of tragedy but specimens with tragic potentialities. In as much as the theater has been turned into a laboratory, so they too have been turned into automata, puppets struggling desperately to be human. They protest—too much perhaps. But in this clinic of humanity their anguished clichés are seen to lack meaningful content; only in their enigmatic but terrible cry, in their very desire to become human, do they transcend this sorry state.

All we are left with is a cry, and the debris of a play. Pirandello's achievement is strangely moving; yet we may well ask why such a paraphernalia of construction yielded results so meager and limited. The humanist critic, we remember, fails to account for the new aesthetic because he is blinkered by a theory of reality which cannot make sense of it. In Pirandello's case, the failure works in reverse.

The humanist assumes that (to use Sartre's image) experience is an onion from which one peels off layers and layers of illusion to expose a small white nub of reality at the center. But if we shift to an existentialist view, we conceive of experience as an unending series of appearances, each of which is equally "real." Pirandello fails, then, because his idealist humanism, from which he ultimately derives his sense of form, cannot contain his existentialist insights.[2] We are left in the end with an impression not of controlled irony, but of bewilderment and contradiction.

The best films of the New Wave leave no such impression. Their existentialism may be partial and muddled but it does support their aesthetic. And since it is this philosophy that their language of smoke and dreams enacts, we need to know its main assumptions. Again, we are summarizing these in note form.

Assumptions of the New Wave

1. A world in which all appearances are equally valid is a world of discontinuity. The self is a series of events without apparent connection: its past and future are a series of actions, but its present is a void waiting to be defined by action. The self therefore is no longer seen as stable. It is without an inner core—without essence. 2. Other people are likewise without essence: since they too are an infinite series of appearances, they remain unpredictable. Only objects, i.e., "things" with an essence, can be understood. People remain mysteries. 3. Since there is no longer a stable reality, traditional moralities prove untrustworthy. They seek to essentialize appearances, order them so that they can be predicted, and so conceal from men their true condition in a discontinuous world—utter isolation. Each is responsible for improvising his moral imperatives; to accept any one role (i.e., to fix one's identity as "bandit," "pianist," or "intellectual") is an evasion of responsibility and becomes "bad faith." Such

---

[2] This failure to embody insights is to be found in a number of directors. In *Rocco*, Visconti fails to find a suitable form for those unmotivated bursts of violence which characterize his anarchistic vision of experience. Since he tries to develop these within the outworn formal husks of nineteenth-century literature, the result is not tragedy but grand opera. Ingmar Bergman, too, cannot find a form for his existentialist insights, and so resigns himself to describing rather than enacting them. His films contain much sophisticated by-play around a philosophy of appearance. They even produce symbols like the clock without hands. Yet the vision remains intellectualized, and the films fail to make their potentially powerful impact.

"bad faith" dehumanizes and turns man into an object. Existentially, he dies.

4. Conversely, to avoid bad faith morality must be an endless, anguished process of improvisation. One no longer acts to fulfill ideals like goodness and decency, but to initiate one's own self-discovery, the only moral "goal" left. Hence action is necessarily opportunistic.

5. In consequence, each act is unique and without social precedence, and so to others will appear motiveless since there is no stable self on which to pin a motive. From this arises the seemingly absurd notion of a motiveless act (*l'acte gratuit*).

6. Our continuous re-creation in every act is the condition of our freedom. But such a continuous freedom demands total responsibility for all that we are, have been, and are to be. It is only theoretically possible to live up to such a rigorous ideal, so that we seek to flee from it into the passivity of being an object. To the man-as-object the world ceases to be an infinite series of appearances and becomes an infinite series of accidents.

The self is a void. Its past and future are a series of events waiting to be filled in. To take on an identity is an act of bad faith: we become objects to be used by others; we die existentially. The hero of *Shoot the Pianist* moves uneasily between such self-destructive roles. He can become Charlie, the timid lover; Edouard Saroyan, the concert pianist; or a wild beast like his brothers. Though he knows that each of these choices is false, he is unable to discover the authentic. In *Breathless* Michel has similarly disastrous alternatives: finding himself cast as bandit, callow lover, or son of an eminent clarinetist, he immediately tries to break out into freedom. Identity is a trap; and since sex is identity, he and Patricia try to save themselves by remaining androgynous. In the void of the self, these identities are deceptions; and they can teach us nothing. They are appearances, as "real" only as the actor's role. To ask if Michel's father was indeed a great clarinetist is as naive and irrelevant as to ask the actor if he was "really" King Lear.

To believe we can learn from the past is also bad faith. Memories are as ambiguous and deceptive as identity. So Sandro cannot learn from his previous *l'avventure*, nor can Charlie make sense of the murder in the snow. Was it a nightmare or did it take place? Such questions are meaningless. If, for the benefit of the doubt, he were to mourn the girl's death—and who knows if she, like Sandro's Anna, ever existed?—he would again be deceiving himself; for to become a mourner is again to take on an identity.

A world of appearances confronts us not with expressive faces and meaningful objects, but with enigmas and indecipherable images.[3] In *Breathless*, Patricia seems to conceal her feelings behind her dark glasses, but when she removes them her face is still an enigma. And it is still the same enigmatic face she turns to us at the end of the film—the face of a beautiful sphinx. To all our questions she returns the same answer: her own cool features into which we can read all meaning or no meaning. The face of Charlie at the end of *Shoot the Pianist* is her male equivalent.

Of all enigmas the most inscrutable is suicide. Because of this inscrutability, and because it is the one act we have no adequate response to, suicide has haunted writers like Fitzgerald and Pavese, film directors like Antonioni and Truffaut. If we mourn a suicide we take on a role, so deceiving ourselves. All we can do is either hastily forget, or answer it with our own enigma. As the hero of *Il Grido* hurls himself down from the tower of a sugar refinery, his wife screams. As with Pirandello's characters, this cry is a last chance to assert her humanity against an inscrutable mystery. She tries to call his bluff by matching enigma against enigma.

In a world of appearances, responsibility lies in discovering one's own morality. Our intention is opportunistic. Since other people are unpredictable, our only chance of survival is to trap them into taking roles. Naturally they will behave in the same way to us. In such a game we can only hope to win by improvising the rules. Our principal trick will be *le gag*, the unpredictable quip or act which turns

---

[3] The process by which morality breaks down into images can be traced most interestingly through the films of Andrzej Wajda. In direct relation to the director's increasing scepticism about their ideology, the plots disintegrate, to be replaced by an unaccounted for lyricism. In *Kanal* plot controls every element of structure, but by *Ashes and Diamonds* it barely contains certain lyrical sequences like the polonaise at dawn. In *Lotna*, his most recent film to be shown here, plot has collapsed completely into a twitter of trivial ironies. The only positive elements left are images—of a white horse, of a flaming emblem—which have no significant connection with the action.

the tables. So Michel robs people, plays jokes on them, and knocks them down. In each case the result is the same: he turns them into objects. "Have you anything against youth?" says a girl and flourishes a copy of *Cahiers.* "Yes," he counters. "I like the old . . ." Distinctions between generations, class, or creed must be minimized: they are traps to be evaded by improvisation.

With Patricia this shadowboxing takes on a disinterested intensity. "A girl's a coward who doesn't light her cigarette the first time," he improvises, and waits for her next move. She bluffs him magnificently by *un acte gratuit;* that is, by an act which is an enigma to him, but which is in terms of her own morality quite understandable. "I stayed with you to see if I were in love. Now I know I am not, and I am no longer interested in you." For the sake of her own freedom he must no longer exist; and it is therefore logical that she should betray him to the police and so indirectly bring about his death. As she says, "Elephants vanish when they are unhappy." Too bad that he should hold the last trump in the pack—death, and an inscrutable remark, *"Tu es dégueulasse."*

A morality which requires us to be continually free and responsible at the same time is impossible; so we retreat into a passivity one of whose forms is stoicism. The world in this position becomes a series of accidents, and we can do nothing about controlling it. Charlie is resigned to bearing his brothers' guilt; because of their crimes he too has become a criminal. Though this transference of guilt is mysterious, he makes no attempt to understand it. He is as stoical about it as he is about the inconsequentiality of life. Somehow for him action and intention never connect. In trying to be kind to the café *patron,* he murders him; respecting women, he kills the two he loves the most. In both this film and in *Breathless* there are long sequences shot from within a car. A jumble of lights and scenery whirl past. The characters look out, but they are cut off from this world, this senseless inanimate place. What can they do about it? Nothing. They shrug their shoulders and drive on.

This morality, of course, applies to more than the story on the screen. It conditions, too, the director's own relationship to his material. He no longer uses the film as a means of unveiling the reality behind illusion. Such penetration is out of place in a world of appearances, in which the cinematic shadows are as "real" as the world outside. If there is no "reality" art cannot be an illusion. Further, the director rejects the rules of filmmaking as bad faith. Both morality and aesthetic must be discovered through improvisation, and our interest will lie in this process of discovery. Each director must create his own language of appearances, although his language is not one of shadows and dreams as Siclier would claim: shadows imply a reflecting object, dreams a waking reality; and these are assumptions rejected by the existentialist. The humanist critic should not be surprised if this improvisation fails to create a plot, for the plot is not now found within the film but in the director's relationship to his material. This is where the conflict and drama lie.

Such an aesthetic is neither new, nor developed to its full extent in the films of Truffaut and Godard. Harold Rosenberg in the *London Magazine* (July 1961) has described how such a theory finds its most extreme form in action painting. The action painter, he writes, does not work from a predetermined idea, but approaches his canvas as he would a person. He sets up a dialogue with his medium, and through improvisation tries to make discoveries about his own mind. "To work from sketches arouses the suspicion that the artist still regards the canvas as a place where the mind records its contents— rather, it is itself the 'mind' through which the painter thinks by changing the surface through paint."

This is not to be seen as a form of self-expression, "which assumes the acceptance of the ego as it is. It has to do with self-creation, self-definition, or self-transcendence." This art is not "personal," though its subject matter is the artist's individual possibilities. Painting here significantly approaches pantomime and dance.[4]

In light of this we must be cautious of the way in which we consider the "content" of *Breathless* and *Shoot the Pianist*. We cannot censure them for the banality of their material or the self-

---

[4] The comparison here with the symbolist aesthetic is irresistible. It is only odd that painting and the cinema should have taken so long to develop similarly. The paradox about this art is that the more successful it is, the more it will appear autonomous. Films like *Breathless* are similar to a symbolist poem in that they try to become an image from which one cannot generalize; and which sets up hazards to our doing so by reminding us that we are controlled by the artist's mind.

regarding nature of their humor. Gags, snippets from the B-feature thriller, Cocteauesque surrealism, and so on, are used not for their intrinsic merit but as a kind of vocabulary. It is only if they fail to find a diction or a style that one can fault their use. We can talk here of burlesque and quotation but not of parody, for parody implies a "real thing" on which to depend.

Since we are not interested in content but in the mind handling it, the disruptions and disconnections of narrative no longer disturb us; for these features do not signal a failure on the director's part but, on the contrary, a success. Failure would lie in his forgetting this self-exploration and becoming involved in the bad faith of telling a tale. He achieves his success by freeing himself from this temptation, imposing his own mental gestures on us. This can best be contrived through camerawork and cutting. In *Shoot the Pianist,* for instance, there is a sequence of a girl walking up and down a corridor which is not edited for the sake of narrative economy, but for that of the maximum visual brilliance. Not enough that this scene, by the canons of traditional filmmaking, should be excessively obtrusive; but Truffaut must underline his pyrotechnics by developing them against a background of virtuoso violin playing. Cutting, too, is used to set up enigmas of troubling beauty. There is one device in particular which is favored by these directors. In *L'Avventura* we see it in embryonic form. It begins in the island hut with a close-up of Claudia's face which fades into a shot of the turbulent sea. Before we can shriek pathetic fallacy, however, the camera pans and we see Claudia in long shot looking down at the waves. Since Antonioni makes no clear point with this device, it remains a trick. Godard, however, uses it continually and to a purpose. Michel raises his revolver to the sun. We cut to a shot of the sun, synchronized (apparently) with the sound of a pistol shot. Then Michel's voice is overlaid: "Women," he says, "never drive carefully." The gun shot has become the crash of car bumpers. At another moment Michel, looking ashamed, is seen in the back of a car. Just when we become certain that he has been arrested, he steps out of the car and pays the driver; and we have to reinterpret his expression. In a world of appearances, Godard seems to be saying, we must always be on our guard; for not only are our assumptions a form of bad faith—they also deceive us.

The director is no longer an interpreter; he is indeed a director, a dictator. Though we may be privileged to enter his mind, we must pay a price in obeying its seemingly arbitrary movements. It is as if we too were inside the fast moving car; for we too have to accept the phantasmagoria outside as the total world. We are all —characters, audience, and film—at the director's mercy. His disturbing treatment of his characters is typical. When Michel turns to us and we see how his dark glasses are without one lens, we laugh uneasily. We are laughing not only at his expense but at the expense of our previous assumptions.

We are not involved in the story, then, but with the director. Each time we try to identify ourselves with the narrative he will deliberately attempt to alienate us. Naturalistic effects therefore must be limited: the love scene is disinfected of possible associations; blood is conspicuously absent from Michel's death. The messiness of the world, all its pathetic and irrelevant demands on our attention, have to be tidied away. If they weren't, our attention might all too easily deviate from the play of the controlling mind.

Our two contradictions are now resolved. Since films like *Breathless* and *Shoot the Pianist* enact a philosophy of discontinuity, they can be disconnected on almost every level and yet cohere beautifully. Further, their improvisations do not appear hesitant, since the director, in making his self-discoveries, uses them purposively. If it is bad faith to believe that reality is predictable, improvisation will be the best way to show us how it is, in fact, a series of appearances in the process of Becoming. At the same time, improvisation rather dishonestly satisfies our naturalistic habits ("It's so like life!") and so dupes us. Too dazzled to notice the aggressive originality of these films, we watch them without our usual defensiveness towards experiment.

PART THREE: THE HUMANIST POSITION RECONSIDERED

Despite its many insights, the Cinema of Appearance is inadequate, for reality is much richer than it makes out. To define its limitations we need a humanism reinterpreted by psycho-

analysis; in the light of which the existentialist outlook is
shown as psychotic and centrality, or the total rich vision, be-
comes closely linked with an idea of the "integrated self."

We have attempted so far to describe the New Cinema without
discussing its own standards of evaluation. How, in fact, would one
of its defenders judge the worth of its film, know whether a film
was good or bad? Their criteria are threefold: firstly, they would be
concerned with the quality of the director's imagination; secondly,
with his ability to avoid the bad faith of previous conventions, like
narrative or plot; and thirdly, with his talent in creating a coherent
style.

By these criteria, *Breathless* emerges as a better film than *Shoot
the Pianist,* for Godard avoids bad faith and creates a self-contained
style whilst Truffaut creates a poignant, uncertain style and hints
at a lost centrality. By evoking an atmosphere similar to the *apache*
world of *Casque d'Or,* Truffaut makes plain his nostalgia for the
lost luminous place where all men are brothers, where love is given
and received with unselfconscious gratitude. In his film the most
haunting image is of people putting arms around each other, helping each other to bear a mutual pain. Behind these images lies a
theme of man's desire for centrality; a theme which is established
from the first moments of the film as Chico, the amiable gangster,
listens to a stranger talking about marriage, and developed through
Charlie, his brother, into a formidable criticism of the Cinema of
Appearance.

As a great pianist, Charlie is unhappy not because his role is a
form of bad faith, but because he knows it hinders him from being
a complete man, from giving himself to others both through his
talents and, especially, through his love for them. This failure is
disastrous. His wife commits suicide when he is unable to give her
the help she needs. As an act of reparation he retreats to a café,
apparent center of brotherhood, where his failure to be a total person leads to the murder of the *patron* and the death of a second girl
he would like to love. Since he cannot be himself, he remains an
enigma to others: people therefore try to create roles for him. The
girl sees him as a means of escape from the sordid city; the *patron*
as a catalyst for lustful fantasies in which all women become prosti-

tutes. Charlie's self-mistrust becomes a denial of responsibility, so
that instead of actions he breeds accidents. It is not without significance that he accidentally kills the *patron* at the moment when he
embraces him; for to claim brotherhood without responsibility can
only lead to death.

In taking refuge from himself in timidity, Charlie condemns himself to failure. Why then has he been forced into such an unhappy
position? The two kidnappers supply an answer. "Always prepare
for the murderer at your door," they say, "and if it turns out to be
only a burglar, you're lucky." In making such a remark, these two
clowns cease to be an arbitrary gag and—unlike the shadowy detectives of *Breathless* with whom Michel and Godard merely play
—take on a sharp symbolic force. They begin to stand for all that
is sordid, stupid, and malignant in society; all that drives Charlie
into flight from society and himself. If we accept this motivation,
we see that Truffaut's film no longer embodies a philosophy of discontinuity, but has become a film about a man who suffers discontinuity and loss.

By existentialist canons, then, and unlike *Breathless*, this film
breaks all the rules and fails. At the same time it approaches more
closely than *Breathless* to our own sense of reality's richness. Since
in the last resort we must base our judgments on this response, we
are forced to question the all-embracing claims of this New Cinema.

The Cinema of Appearance, we see, is a retreat from a total vision
of reality. Though this retreat is honest (it takes courage to realize
how lonely man is in a disconnected world where traditional con-
solations are useless), it is unable to articulate our sense of life's
richness. Yet to argue failure in such terms is to leave oneself vulnerable to the charge of whimsical subjectivism. We need a public
criterion. One of these is indicated by psychoanalysis, though this
does not exclude others.

The terms we would use are those of Melanie Klein. According
to her, the individual under stress moves either towards integration
or disintegration—and this, of course, conditions his perception of
the world. To achieve integration, he must work through the de-
pressive (or mourning) phase in which he acknowledges, however
unknowingly, the fact that he has destroyed his inner world by

envy. By confronting this desolation, he begins to re-create the value and coherence of his inner world, and this in turn begins to give meaning to the outer world. If this desolation is too hard to bear, however, he will defend himself by "splitting" himself, and thus cutting off the consciousness of depression. If he does this frequently he gradually becomes schizophrenic. The inner and outer world cease to relate and each in turn splits more and more.

By this view, *Breathless* exhibits all the symptoms of such a manic defense. It is no more than a splintered fragment of a splintered reality. Its hard, glossy clarity can be seen as an attempt to foil the onrush of reality with all its messy completeness. It constructs a relationship whose sole justification is to deny love, with its mutual knowledge and commitment, and substitutes instead a form of manic defense—narcissism—so that Michel and Patricia see each other as mirrors and not as people. It works towards no release, because it creates no solid, intractable stuff through which to work. The disturbing tensions between youth and age, class and creed, are deliberately excluded. Bodies never sweat. Objects hit, neither crunch nor thump. Hence death is denied its sole human significance—loss. For as there is nothing to lose, there is nothing to gain; as there is nothing to destroy, there is nothing to create. This is the antiart of an antiworld; and all we are left to marvel at is the pyrotechnic flight of intellect through void.

Or so the director would have us believe. Yet even the most extreme manic defense is not impregnable. In *Shoot the Pianist* there is, obviously, a fumbling attempt to re-create a world where love and the desolation of reality are not feared. In *Breathless* the break in the defence is not so immediately apparent. It only begins to reveal itself when we look closely at its morality, which is a form of stoicism.[5]

Since traditional moralities have lost their sanctions, our only alternatives are either collapse or a manifestation of dignity simply at the process of being. This stoicism finds for itself a weird code of honor which runs counter to the improvised rules of the game.

---

[5] Without a public morality our feelings lack sanction, and we become hesitant about their importance. Consequently we play them down: we develop a morality which is "cool." Our repressed energy, in compensation, finds release in violence, in living for "kicks."

Michel, having murdered, must court death and endure without comment the neon headlines announcing his coming capture. Patricia, having betrayed, must go on betraying. As Michel says, "Murderers murder, informers inform, and lovers love." Michel imitates the tough man ethos—his idol is Humphrey Bogart—and mimes his set of aggressive gestures, which is ridiculous since a shadow world presents no objects. There is no point in being tough if there is nothing to be tough about. If this stoicism is inconsistent with the theory of the world as appearance, why then does Michel subscribe to it?

In Kleinian terms one would say it was a defense against the tragic sense of life, of the fullness which love and gratitude can bring, and with it—since we cannot have one without the other—the desolation of death and destruction. One can only partially realize this knowledge, for a complete realization would require more than human courage. To some degree we all have our defenses; and all our defenses in the light of this reality are absurd. Michel's stoicism, however, is a defense not only against this awareness of tragedy but against the terrifying demands made by an existentialist morality; for this philosophy of appearance is in itself deeply psychotic. Instead of mourning it offers anguish, instead of the integrated self it offers flight from identity, and instead of reality it offers us a reality like a shattered mirror.

Yet Michel and Patricia cannot gag the tragic sense. It is there in the pregnancy they try to ignore, and it is there in Michel's desire to go to Rome, that old center where all roads used to lead. It is even there in his jealousy, which contradicts his "cool" creed of stoic indifference. A sense of loss does issue from this film as a note of wistfulness—the willfulness of world-baffled children. And once we have caught this note, we begin to make sense of the film in humanist terms. However tentatively, the film begins to transform itself and take on the shape of drama. It begins to manifest plot. Up to now we have accepted Patricia's betrayal of Michel on its own terms as an *acte gratuit*. It now exposes itself to a different reading.

Throughout the film Patricia is bombarded with a series of misleading, gnomic, and contradictory statements about the meaning of life. There is a spate of these at her airport interview with a celebrity. Finally she manages to get in her own question, which is both urgent and, in the context, rather stupid. "What is your greatest ambition?" she asks. Though his reply—"to become immortal, and then to die"—might pass as an artist's insolent flourish, it cannot help her; and help is what she needs. Patricia is forced into fabricating naive formulae so that she can cope with life. In order to be independent of men, she claims, she has to earn a living. Yet she is waiting for some lead which she cannot discover. Her American friend baffles her with remarks she cannot understand about books she only boasts of having read. She would like to love Michel, but he makes her play his game which drains words of their meaning. Perhaps her hand really shook with emotion when she could not light her cigarette for the first time, but the rules force her to "gag" back at the accusation. Michel might be sincere about his Rome invitation, but how is she to judge when he won't allow her to know him? He denies her the full choice of commitment and rejection and uses her simply to explore the spectrum of his own attitudes.

All she can do is retaliate. Her betrayal is a desperate attempt to force him to commit himself either one way or another. But he denies her even this gratification by the enigma of his death. She is left, at last, still unenlightened, still not knowing whether she is a sex machine waiting to be worked, or a woman waiting to be loved. Not knowing who she is, she cannot tell us; and so, in the final shot, she looks out at us enigmatically. Yet in psychoanalytic terms the enigma does betray a meaning. For is this not the face of the seventeen-year-old schizophrenic described by R. D. Laing in *The Divided Self*, in whom, beneath the vacancy and terrible placidity of the catatonic trance, there still lurked the desolation of irreparable loss, and of whom, though she was a hopeless case, the author could still conclude: "There was a belief (however psychotic a belief it was, it was still a form of faith in something of great value in herself) that there was something of great worth deeply lost or buried inside her, as yet undiscovered by herself or by anyone. If one could go deep into the depths of the dark sea one would discover the bright gold, or if one could get fathoms down one would discover the pearl at the bottom of the sea."?

·∘❨ REVIEWS ❩∘·

ALAIN VARGAS

❖◈❖◈❖◈❖◈❖◈❖◈❖◈❖◈❖◈❖◈❖◈❖◈❖◈❖◈❖◈❖◈❖◈❖◈❖◈❖

Pierre Braunberger presents Charles Aznavour in a film by François Truffaut, adapted from David Goodis's *Shoot the Piano Player*.*

Thus begin, almost to the last detail, the credits of the second full-length film by the *auteur* of *The 400 Blows*.

Why *Shoot the Piano Player?* In the first place, by and for Charles Aznavour. When Truffaut had a presentiment of the distinctive character—something between a James Dean and a Charlie Chaplin —that this composer/singer could become, he had not yet abandoned film criticism, that last resort that isn't even a means of subsistence. Truffaut had this vision even though Aznavour was highly controversial and considered incapable of playing comic roles, according to the generally held definition of comedy; an attitude that is really meaningless, since what good is acting, or worse, knowing how to act, when it's essentially a question of being alive?

In the second place, the movie was made for David Goodis, Truffaut's favorite detective story writer. Hardly had Truffaut read *Piano Player* than a fantastic **runa**way car scene seized his imagination, and he thought immediately of Aznavour to play it.

La Tête contre les murs and *Les Drageurs* thus must have satisfied Truffaut, insofar as Aznavour was a revelation to even the most blasé or sceptical eyes, but they also must have disappointed him insofar as Franju (who nevertheless has the honor of really having helped Aznavour make his screen debut) and Mocky were

Translated from Cinéma 1960, *no. 44 (March 1960): 31–35. Copyright © 1960 by* Cinéma 1960. *Reprinted by permission of the publishers.*

* [*Down There* was published in France under the title *Tirez sur le pianiste* —Ed.]

using him in only one key, hieratic or clownlike, according to the situation. No matter what differences there are between them, there was in some way in Aznavour the material of a Sinatra.

And so it was that "Charlie, 32 years old, a piano player," hard and vulnerable, resembling both a clown and a Franciscan monk, becomes active rather than passive, seduces women instead of being seduced, and drives others to suicide instead of being suicidal. To like an actor is quite simply a matter of wanting to reveal him to himself, while revealing him simultaneously to the public, in an entirely new, unexpected light. The filming of several scenes that I was able to watch, and the rushes I saw, inclined me to think that both of them have already profited. I would bet that words like heartrending, poetic, charismatic, and pathetic will certainly appear again and again in the writings of our high-flown critics as the four qualities that best describe the performance of my friend Charlie, as the father of Zazie would say.

Truffaut initially had hoped to film *Shoot the Piano Player* entirely in the studio, following the example of Visconti's *White Nights,* which had fascinated him so. But he abandoned this idea after seeing the cost of stage models, scenery, transparencies, etc., triple his projected budget. During the six weeks between Pigalle and not place Blanche but place de Levallois, from the Prisunic to the Hotel d'Orsay, all the images of *Piano Player* were shot in Dyaliscope black and white by Raoul Coutard, that adventurer in Cameflex who photographed *La Passe du diable* and the newest film of the New Wave, Jean-Luc Godard's *Breathless.*

The script that Truffaut uses here is similar to that of *The 400 Blows:* both have almost no technical directions. Nevertheless one can't totally accept the criticism-manifesto he made about the admirable *Passions Juveniles,* although it's an excellent brief for what he's done himself: ". . . the direction is largely improvised, full of ideas that were unpredictable before filming, and obviously so spontaneous that one wouldn't know how to indicate them in a script." As spontaneous as his improvisations may appear to an unprepared spectator, they are born in the fire of rehearsals or successive takes, and thus frequently at least are very premeditated. Only the person who wishes to be mystified will be.

Truffaut is more relaxed than he had been for *The 400 Blows.*

Not that he had been in an impossible mood then, but now he no longer risks his career on a first full-length film; he does not have to direct children in this film; and he has a certain confidence derived from the public and critical success of *The 400 Blows* (acclaimed by people as diverse as Buñuel, Rossellini, Franju, Welles, Gene Kelly, Lang, Resnais, Cocteau, Renoir, Becker), all of which relieved him of certain worries.

But does this mean that *Piano Player*—a work of relaxation between *The 400 Blows,* which he had inside him for so long before he unburdened himself, and *Le Bleu d'outre-tombe* (*The Blue Beyond the Grave*) (for and by Jeanne Moreau, in June), which is presently his most cherished project—will be more the work of a director than an *auteur?*

No, despite whatever its . . . *auteur* may say or think. Truffaut, in fact, will never make anything but autobiographical films. I don't mean films in which he will describe his life—Antoine Doinel/ Jean-Pierre Léaud is and is not the adolescent Truffaut was—but films in which he *will speak only about what he knows and likes.*

Thus *Piano Player*'s script alludes to those quotation-homages with which Truffaut likes to season his films, as he used to season his articles: here a line of Sacha Guitry and Félix Leclerc, there André Bazin and Max Ophuls.

Thus *Piano Player,* like *The 400 Blows* before and *Jules and Jim* later (once again Jeanne Moreau), will exalt a *cult of friendship* under the guise of fraternity—one of the keys to François Truffaut the man in both his public and private lives, despite the slanderous legend of his unpleasantly careerist nature. His friends would attest to this without any obligation; it wouldn't be the first time that a hypersensitive person is accused of heartlessness, nor would he be the first sufferer to be called cold-blooded.

Thus *Piano Player* will demonstrate, with disquieting yet warm insistence, a great truth: Truffaut's inner alliance of intimacy and genuine poetic realism; the *moral* and *epidermal* relations of a timid, unstable, maladjusted (shall I say characterial?) man with several women; the slow and unavoidable disintegration of a couple whose driving element, the man, passes from semipoverty to wealth, from semipenury to opulence, and from semianonymity to celebrity.

You can read in the details of *Piano Player* Truffaut's love for music halls. From the Alhambra to the Cheval d'Or, passing through les Trois-Baudets or Bobino, there is no club or bar that he doesn't visit regularly. After movies he loves music halls best in the entire world. He confided in me one day that if it happened for some reason or another that he could no longer be involved in films (either as a critic or a director), he would like to write a music-hall column. It was there in a music hall, in a cabaret,[1] that he decided to cast Jean Constantin as his composer (*The 400 Blows, Shoot the Piano Player*); also from cabarets came the actors Charles Aznavour, Pierre Repp, and Henri Virlogeux (the English teacher and the night watchman in *The 400 Blows,* in which Dufhilo, another cabaret person, had a scene cut out in the editing); and Serge Davri, "Plyne the tightwad," an astonishing character, the counterpart of Jean Hersholt (the informer in *Greed*), and dish breaker emeritus; and Boby La Pointe, whose light and vulgar songs will be hummed all over after *Piano Player*. The following excerpts from "Vanilla and Raspberry" give the reader only a weak idea of the extraordinary uneven rhythm that gives them both charm and strength:

> She had few advantages
> And wanted more
> She had them added
> At a beauty store
> Ah Ah Ah!
> In Maine and Loire
> They shape your breast like a pear
> And at a clinic in Anger
> They operate, no danger
> Whether you're a young or an old thing
> They can change almost everything
> Except what you can't change
> What an insult!

[1] "Formerly, the best school for actors was the café-concert. Today there are no more café-concerts, but it's in the cabarets, the many nightclubs, that you can unearth the stars of the future. And the touring company, with its precarious way of life when it has a young troupe, is the best place to meet the movie stars of tomorrow." (Jean Renoir, recently.)

Ah, vanilla and raspberry
Are the breasts of destiny
Poum Poum!*

Also around Charles Aznavour will be Michèle Mercier (Clarisse),
whom the former critic of *Arts* [Truffaut] was the first to praise
in her first screen appearance (*Retour de Manivelle*); Nicole Berger
(Théresa), shown here as never before; Marie Dubois (Léna), former
pupil of Henri Rollan at the Conservatory, discovered on television,
named by Audiberti, and a new star people will talk about;
Catherine Lutz (Mammy), whom all the BBC projection room reg-
ulars know very well; Albert Rémy, Richard Kanayan, and Jacques
Aslanian (Charlie's brothers); Claude Heyman (the impresario);
Alex Joffé; and finally, the "American stars," saving the best for
last, the duo of killers, Daniel Boulanger, the ubu-esque cop from
Breathless, the script and dialogue writer for *The Love Game*
(formerly *Suzanne et les roses*), the first feature by Philippe de Broca,
produced by Chabrol; and Claude Mansard, right now the best
French-made actor and the fetish of the new lords, since he's been
seen in *The Lovers, La Tête contre les murs, The 400 Blows,* and
Breathless.

* [I am sorry that the lack of a transcript of the English-language version of
Shoot the Piano Player prevents me from here reprinting with a lavish tribute
the lyrics of this song as translated by Noelle Gillmor. The wit of the subtitles and the obvious care the translator has taken with them constitutes one
of the less obvious but most pleasant surprises for a first viewer of the film.—
ED.]

PIERRE KAS

❖❖◗

A few years ago a ciné-club whose name I can't remember had the idea of organizing a debate on the basic relationship between form and matter in cinema. The aspect of pure logic in this formulation disguised rather poorly their desire to emphasize the "content" of films. To simplify things, let's call it the subject. At the meeting a simple question was asked: what is subject matter? Alexandre Astruc rose and said: "If I want to film pride, is that a subject?"

Many years and many films separate us from this violently animated discussion. The polemic has a smell of the museums. However, after a second viewing of *Shoot the Piano Player*, and still literally enchanted by so much grace, it seemed to me that this film demonstrates very strikingly the ascendancy of subject matter over the unraveling of plot. I certainly could not recount the story in a sentence, but it is very clear that François Truffaut has filmed timidity as it has never been done before.

People have said a little too quickly that Truffaut chose a detective story only as a pretext. Goodis's book is, in fact, a good detective novel. Perhaps aficionados don't rate Goodis as highly as William P. MacGivern, Chester Himes, or Charles Williams, but finally, who knows . . . I don't find anything arbitrary in his choice, and I see very well what basic modesty dictated it. It's as if, after *The 400 Blows*, Truffaut had felt the need to take a certain

Translated from "L'Âme du canon," Cahiers du Cinéma, *no. 115 (January 1961): 44–46. Copyright © 1961 by* Les Editions de l'Etoile. *Reprinted by permission of* Les Editions de l'Etoile *and Grove Press, Inc.*

distance and impose a certain discipline on himself. A real *auteur* doesn't necessarily explain himself alone, nor does he necessarily take all his material from his own background. We live in such a confusion of logic that we have a natural tendency to apply rigid definitions mechanically, without seeing that the contours are often changing and in flux.

In reality, Truffaut's modesty before the outlines of his second film resembles Gide's definition of classical art: searching first of all for the commonplace in order precisely that it not be banal, and finding its greatest liberty in the midst of external constraint. Behind the façade of imposed events, everything in *Piano Player* happens as if the expression of personality had become more perceptible to the viewer; as if, within the framework of an externally imposed detective story plot, the individuality of the characters became therefore all the more apparent.

But no doubt it's a great betrayal of the film to wander in the meandering ways of a changing logic, when the first, the most durable, and the most persistent impression the film gives is one of charm. Charm is the equivalent of grace for a work of art. I would happily put myself out to give a definition of grace. It's like style: you have it or you don't; if you look for it, you'll never have it; there's no way to get it, to rent it, or to buy it. Unless you try different kinds of magic. *Shoot the Piano Player* has more charm than any film I've seen for years. But, do I mean that therefore it's impossible to guess the reasons why?

One is obviously the freedom of narrative. That's a paradox for a story with a detective plot. Ten examples of admirable American detective films can be cited where the iron rule of plot gives birth to a conception of the *useful*. Everything is sacrificed to effectiveness. Most French films that aspire to this genre are caricatures of the method. In *Shoot the Piano Player* it seems to me that plot, without disappearing, passes into the background to the profit of the characters and their relationships with each other. One important example of this is the transformation of the enemies and killers, who inflict the plot on the charming heroes, into grotesque and comic villains. Like the horrible circumstances of life, they had to be laughable because in the film they represent the plot against poetry. The visual beauty of the end, in the snow, the emotion that the heroine's death inspires, isn't diminished but magnified in counterpoint to these grotesque gangsters; these maladroit machine gunners, who between the two of them fail to hit anything at six feet but accurately hit love in the heart at thirty feet.

The quality of acting, of course, is another reason. The ins and outs of timidity, its broken or entombed spirits, from now on have Aznavour's face. Here is an exceptional coming together of an actor and his purpose, the intelligence of a character and the most solid instincts of the person who plays him. But the demanding sweetness of Marie Dubois, the simple and cordial eroticism of Michèle Mercier, the extraordinary authority of Nicole Berger, all support and augment the enchantment we discover. Naturally it is clear that Truffaut has loved his characters infinitely, that he has taken every care to help them live. Direction of actors certainly begins there. But after reading Julien Duvivier's recent contemptuous declarations about actors, I have asked myself many questions about the relationship between a director and his actors. There's no general law about anything in film at any level. Everything is a particular case. Let those people who like to beat, order, deceive, lie, show contempt, scream, or give rules (since it's so true that only results count), be pleased with what they do. But what results? Why? For whom? I don't say that the results Clouzot gets are bad. They can be. But I totally contest the existence and the praise of Clouzot's method. And now let's talk about charm . . .

I wonder if, in fact, I believe that Truffaut's secret is that he loves not only his characters but also the actors who incarnate his characters. I'm not creating a theory; I don't say that's what you have to do, or that everyone has to do it. Besides, everyone can't. But it seems to me that that's what Truffaut has done. So much freedom, so much flexibility, so much relaxation, properly engender a certain rigor in the acting. Yes, I think that you can get these things only by loving them, and in return the gifts given by each actor are made more easily.

The flexibility of the shooting script and the direction, so sketchy in *Les Mistons* and *The 400 Blows,* is fully achieved here. It furnishes a kind of sureness of effect that comes, as with the direction of actors, from Truffaut's feeling for the others in the film. Many other things count too, the music, the songs. But in as much as I

have listed the elements of proved charms, I have the impression
that I have forgotten the essence.

We have to reason by analogy, a sinister process. I thought at
first that the essence of the film was the tone, until the moment
when I said to myself that it was like the effect of the sleep-pro-
ducing virtue of opium, or phlogiston. There is no tone in itself,
apart from a certain vision of things. A catastrophic or aggressive
vision of human relations could not be asserted on the basis of a
charming tone. First the bitterness, the suffering before the atroc-
ity of conversations, then the entertainment, the taste for the
baroque, the restrained compassion, the taste for wandering, the
taking of one's time—all finally characterize *Shoot the Piano Player*.
Charm and kindness are finally what I believe to be the qualities
of its author. This is really funny if you think about the reputation
Truffaut has cut out for himself in the cinema business, the number of broken windows. It's funny but not absurd, because it's not
surprising that a timid and demanding love of movies has been
taken for spitefulness and aggressiveness. Cinema, strangely enough,
has a strong morality: in a blinding way one sees who *is* the author,
what he's worth in every sense. Let's say that his soul is visible.

Analogically, I looked for a literary equivalent to these qualities
of film, a kind of close example, maybe even a false one. This special
mixture, this alliance of burlesque and tenderness, for my taste,
also characterizes "Pierrot, mon ami" or "Un rude hiver." I count
Queneau as the greatest living French writer or, let's say, without
making up some ridiculous hierarchy, that there's no one I like
better.

Even by the subterfuge of an analogy, I'm happy to be able to
place in the wake of Queneau the two films I've liked best in a
long time, *Zazie dans le metro* and *Shoot the Piano Player*. The
novels and the films may be different, but it's in their differences
that things are worthwhile.

Enchantment? Here we have it.

MARCEL MARTIN

◆◇◆

Waiting now for the reception of his first film since he received the prize for direction at Cannes in 1959 for *The 400 Blows,* François Truffaut risks seeing himself summarily executed with the release of *Shoot the Piano Player,* for good reasons as well as bad ones.

The good reasons, or at least the seemingly good ones, assert that the subject of *Shoot the Piano Player* will seem narrower and more frivolous after *The 400 Blows.* On this point Truffaut explains himself perfectly in the following interview,* and he does it with such evident conviction that no one could think to reproach him with wanting to remain the prisoner of a genre nor force his inspiration and his talent to attack the great problems of the day. It is certainly normal that critics and the enlightened public both want to find in films the reflection of their political, social, and humane preoccupations. It's one of the most frequent reproaches that has reasonably been made to the New Wave—that they forget we are in 1960, that grave problems have been posed to us today, and that the cinema must not be only a means of escape, under pain of becoming sterile.

Certainly, with this point of view, there will be a general disappointment with *Shoot the Piano Player.* And yet one has to admit that the universal and unanimous success of *The 400 Blows* has been a little unexpected. It is evident that the film has completely escaped from its director and is repeatedly crowned in private by

Translated from "Le Pianiste de Truffaut," Cinéma 61, *no. 52 (January 1961): 5–7. Copyright © 1961 by* Cinéma 61. *Reprinted by permission of* Cinéma 61.

* [See pp. 133–37, ED.]

groups that one does not expect to find so enthusiastic, but who have the habit of "annexation." That the film has had the Catholic International Office of Cinema prize bestowed on it at Cannes, and more recently the Grand Prize of the Week of Religious Cinema at Valladolid, did not fail to embarrass, if not to surprise, those who found in *The 400 Blows* a tone of bruised tenderness and an almost hopeless distress and those who had seen in it, in any case, more a cry of anarchist revolt than a breviary of moral edification.

I don't think that François Truffaut wanted this. You might say that this moving film, once it left him, after a creative act of undoubted sincerity, truly escaped from him and took on an unforeseen importance and resonance. And, therefore, it's not bad that *Shoot the Piano Player* will disappoint all those who burnt incense before *The 400 Blows,* and, for the bad reasons I've just pointed out, attempted to imprison the author in a conformist but edifying universe that is clearly not his own.

Be assured that these same people, after they detest his second film because it doesn't correspond to their expectations, will be blind to the unbounded sensibility and especially the remarkable sense of cinema that it shows. Such a film clearly offers us, by methods far removed from those of a Resnais or a Godard, moments of intense and profound cinematic pleasure. I am not far, myself, from preferring it to *The 400 Blows* for precisely this reason of pleasure, and for something else in addition, which may be surprising but I hope the spectator will think about: *Shoot the Piano Player* contains fewer commercial formulas and less glibness—"commercial" isn't a pejorative judgment but a statement of fact—than *The 400 Blows. The 400 Blows* had everything necessary to attract a vast public; *Shoot the Piano Player,* I'm afraid, will only please the true lover of movies.

François Truffaut says that he wished to make his film an homage to the American B-film. And certainly he got closer to those films not only by his subject (taken from a detective novel by David Goodis), but also, on the brilliant and detached side, by Truffaut's ability to go beyond and transfigure his subject by extremely careful direction and especially, let me say again, by a sense of cinema that appears in the unusual intensity of his magisterial use of Cinemascope, in the poetry of the camera movement and the dissolves, by the fascinating presences of Aznavour and Nicole Berger—in a word, by a "charm," in the strongest sense of the word, that is freed from any images and situations that deny the lightness and the detachment of his purpose.

Truffaut tells us: "I wished to make a respectful pastiche of the lesser American cinema." He has succeeded perfectly, but it's clear that one must love the "lesser American cinema" if one is to love his film. I mean that one must sometimes look on the screen not for a Cartesian story that leads to a demonstrable conclusion, but for isolation and action, and especially a little dream and fantasy, a little vertigo, and a little poetry.

What I've said here doesn't constitute proper and well-formed "criticism." I have no other aim than to prepare the spectator to sample a film that will not win the Grand Prize at Cannes, but which will delight the real connoisseurs.

STANLEY KAUFFMANN

◆◆◆

François Truffaut's *Shoot the Piano Player* was made before *Jules and Jim*; the reception of the latter has apparently prompted the importation of the former. It is welcome, too, although on a smaller scale it has the same proportion of shortcomings to virtues as the other film. Truffaut's public statements contain lots of blithe assertions: "I'm lazy, and when the day for shooting a film arrives, I don't have a finished script . . . I may find myself changing my notions about what I want to do right in the middle of making a

From A World On Film (*New York: Harper and Row, 1962*), *pp. 230–32. First published in* The New Republic, *July 9, 1962. Copyright © 1962 by Stanley Kauffmann. Reprinted by permission of Harper & Row, Publishers, Inc., and Brandt and Brandt.*

film. And on days when I'm feeling merry, I shoot merry scenes, and on my gloomy days I shoot gloomy ones." These utterances would be affectation except that the finished films bear him out. They really do have an air of improvisation, and they burst into blossoms of high jinks or intensity, sometimes quite irrelevant to story and previous mood.

For example, this film opens with a man running down dark streets, fleeing pursuers. He rams into a lamppost and is helped to his feet by a passing stranger. He then walks a couple of blocks with the stranger who chats with him about his wife. They shake hands and part; then the brother visits the hero and the film begins. The street encounter was the kind of intimacy that can occur between strangers, and it has an excursive charm which (as with some moments in *Jules and Jim*) Truffaut simply felt like pursuing, that's all.

The rewards of this free-verse approach are ample if the director can support it with warm invention and cool skill. Truffaut has plenty of both. The disadvantage is that the net effect is patchy and tends to detract from the subject matter. Recently a dinner companion told me that when he was in London in the thirties, he went to a midnight movie and saw a feature film that started with a costume sequence, then had a snatch of a musical, then a chunk of a gangster picture, and so on. He thought he was drowsy and was just not following. Next day he was told that the British quota laws of the time made it mandatory to show a domestic feature at least once a day with every foreign feature. In order to exhibit profitable Hollywood pictures, the English studios would sweep an hour-and-a-half's worth of bits off their own cutting-room floors, paste them together and, to satisfy the law, would run them off at midnight when no one was expected to see them.

Their solution is a *reductio ad absurdum* of the Truffaut method. In the midst of a kidnapping scene, the criminals get into an avuncular discussion about first names with the young victim. When a hood says that if he's lying, he hopes his mother drops dead, an inset shot shows his mother dropping dead. All these touches are funny or moving, but we sometimes wonder whether we've dozed off and missed a transition.

The film is based on an American crime novel, the genre that many French intellectuals glorify, particularly the group around the magazine *Cahiers du Cinéma,* for which Truffaut used to be a critic. It is an imitation Humphrey Bogart vehicle, and the film's paradox is that Truffaut weakens the suspense with his digressive gusto, yet that gusto is the best element in it. The hybrid result is neither a tight crime story nor a sound crime satire like Huston's *Beat the Devil.* But there are fine sequences. The scene in which the hero and the "nice" girl go to bed for the first time compresses a long passionate day into a two-minute poem, beautifully composed.

Charles Aznavour, the pianist-hero, reticent and small, may do for short men what Ezio Pinza did a decade ago for middle-aged men: make them popular sex images. There are three competent young actresses in the film, Marie Dubois, Nicole Berger, and Michèle Mercier, the last of whom seems much too lovely to be a low-priced tart.

BOSLEY CROWTHER

◈◈◈

François Truffaut, the French director who showed in *The 400 Blows* that he had a rare talent for lacing pathos with slapstick comedy, pulled all the stops on that talent and let it run rampant when he made *Shoot the Piano Player,* which arrived at the Fifth Avenue Cinema yesterday.

Nuttiness, pure and simple—nuttiness of the sort that has a surly kidnapper in a presumably serious scene swearing to something on the life of his mother, whereupon there's a cut to the mother dropping dead—surges and swirls through the tangle of

From The New York Times, *July 24, 1962.* © *1962 by The New York Times Company. Reprinted by permission.*

solemn intimations in this film until one finds it hard to see or figure what M. Truffaut is about.

Evidently he is asking that the audience pay gentle heed to the significance of the old barroom legend, "Don't shoot the piano player; he is doing the best he can." For his hero is a small piano player in a noisome Parisian bar who turns out to be a poignant victim of fate and his own timidity.

This little ivory-tickler, played by Charles Aznavour with an almost Buster Keaton-like insistence on the eloquence of the dead pan, is more than a tired and pallid jangler of popular ragtime tunes. Oh, yes. He is a former concert pianist with a brilliant and glamorous past. But for some unspecified reason he couldn't get along with his wife, who finally tells him she brought him his big chance with her virtue, and this dumps him into the bars.

Maybe, in this little fellow, M. Truffaut is trying to construct an arch example of a sentimental hero that he is subtly attempting to spoof. But if this is the case, why does he bear down on the little fellow's piety so hard and bring his serio-comic roughhouse to a mawkishly tearful end? Why does he scramble his satire with a madly melodramatic plot and have the little piano player kill a man in defense of a girl?

It looks, from where we are sitting, as though M. Truffaut went haywire in this film, which he made as his second feature picture, following the great success of *The 400 Blows*. It looks as though he had so many ideas for movie outpouring in his head, so many odd slants on comedy and drama and sheer clichés that he wanted to express, that he couldn't quite control his material, which he got from a novel by David Goodis called *Down There*.

Else why would he switch so abruptly from desperately serious scenes and moods to bits of irrelevant nonsense or blatant caricature? Why would he let Nicole Berger play a lengthy, heartbreaking scene in which she boldly explains to her husband how she was unfaithful to him, then turn around a few minutes later and put two gangsters through a frolic of farce?

It is a teasing and frequently amusing (or moving) film that M. Truffaut has made, but it simply does not hang together. It does not find a sufficiently firm line, even one of calculated spoof or mischief, on which to hang and thus be saved.

M. Aznavour is touching as the hero, when he is supposed to be, but his character is much too shallow and vagrant for substantiality. Marie Dubois is appealing as a young barmaid who tries to help him out, and Mlle. Berger is excellent in her brief role as his flashback wife. Several other fellows overact in various roles. The English subtitles do bare justice to the lusty colloquial French.

·◦❊ ESSAYS ❊◦·

The Sensitive Spot
by JEAN-PAUL TÖRÖK

Incidentally, the same David Goodis who wrote *Dark Passage* has also written a very beautiful novel, which it's not necessary to have read. It would, however, be necessary to stop those who didn't show up with *Down There* in hand from seeing *Shoot the Piano Player*. This precaution would save having to see the film more than twice. Relieved of the worry of transposing to the screen a story he certainly liked reading, François Truffaut would be allowed to move immediately to the main point, in company with the small number of viewers who are concerned with the things that concern him.

But at the outset there was David Goodis's really beautiful novel, which Truffaut really had to adapt, and adapted faithfully, to make a film whose major part was necessarily devoted to a persistent destruction of the novel. And it has been destroyed so well that *Down There* retains little more than an "accompanying" relation to *Shoot the Piano Player,* a curious state of affairs, since they do tell the same story.

In the suburbs of a large city, in a shabby little bar, a man plays the piano. He's a former virtuoso, an idol of the music-mad public, who mysteriously disappeared one day, changed his name and personality to strand himself in this suburban cabaret, unknown to anyone else. He appears very concerned with not attracting attention, to obliterate himself as much as possible. One night his brother, a low-grade gangster he hasn't seen for many years, bursts

Translated from "Le Point Sensible," Positif, *no. 38 (March 1961):* *39–47. Copyright © 1961 by Éditions du Terrain Vague. Reprinted by permission of* Positif.

into the bar. Hunted by two killers, he's come to ask for help. The piano player refuses. He doesn't want to get involved in anything. However, at the last minute, in spite of himself, he makes up his mind and by a ridiculous but effective action saves his brother from his pursuers. The pursuers notice the complicity of the two men, discover their relationship, and beat up the piano player so that he'll reveal his brother's hiding place. Understanding that the musician is in trouble, the waitress at the cabaret, who secretly loves him, joins up with him, and the two of them find themselves caught in the usual gears of this kind of novel. The piano player will commit a murder; the waitress will be killed in the final shoot-out.

Truffaut has repeated enough times that the scenario had no importance. Nevertheless Goodis's novel being what it is, any director who would have been satisfied with translating it into images with a minimum of ambitions could have brought off a very good film. That's a very obvious proposition that a first viewing of *Shoot the Piano Player* immediately challenges.

FIRST VIEWING

The remaking of a "thriller" type film today is of interest only as a retrospective. In spite of some rare American survivals, the genre is quite dead, and commendable efforts—Cornfield, Lerner— to renew it by reducing it to its essence result only in fastidious exercises in style, in the functioning without surprise of a skeletal mechanism. With rare exceptions—Ralph Habib's admirable *Escapade,* which only *Positif* noted when it came out—the thriller could never adapt itself to France, that bastion of antiromanticism, except at the price of sacrilegious distortions that resulted in the proliferation of "the detective story," good of their kind, characterized by the loathsome uniformity of the family table, where the cops and the baddies swill beer between two disillusioned shoot-outs. Nevertheless, let's do Truffaut the favor of believing that he could have, if he wanted to, produced an arresting stylistic exercise an homage to the American authors of the great period. Whatever you say, you have at least to recognize his courage to have preferred a solution of continuity to one of facility: *Shoot the Piano Player* is not a *film noir* any more; the rules and conventions of the genre are systematically destroyed, not with the casual contempt of the man who is very high-handed with his subject (Chabrol and Stanley Elkin's *A double tour*), but destroyed from the *inside* by a director who first wants to free himself from anything that could tie him to a subject he knows is a fine one, but from which he must nevertheless break loose so he can do *something else*; so he can say freely what he wants to say. Truffaut doesn't play at the cultivated aesthete who, annoyed at having to "deliver a message" by using a "popular" novel (movies are an industry, aren't they?), and wants above all to show he isn't a dupe, hurries through the plot and generally ruins the film. On the contrary, if Truffaut judges it necessary to destroy the original work, he does it honestly, in complicity with his author, scrupulously adapting the novel, keeping the special natures of the characters, the greater part of the dialogue, the feeling of the situations, and even the part-tender, part-ironic "tone" of the description. But he recaptures them *on his own terms* by so subtly bending the narrative that, by an artifice worthy of Borges, even David Goodis's text becomes François Truffaut's text. Insidiously substituting himself for the American writer, Truffaut accomplishes the exact opposite of an adaptation: he lives in the heart of the novel and "possesses" it (in the magical sense of the word). For him the novel has become above all a state of soul.

So, since the "letter" of *Down There* has been loyally respected, it's not so much the "spirit" that's been modified, as the principal characteristics of the "genre noir," particularly its efficiency. Truffaut shifts and disorients the perspective, and puts the viewer in an uncomfortable state where the usual points of reference have abruptly vanished. *Shoot the Piano Player* begins traditionally: a man flees in the night; there are automobile lights, moving shadows, panting. But he unluckily bumps his head into a streetlamp and falls stunned. An honest bourgeois (Alex Joffé), who is passing by, a bouquet of flowers in hand, charitably helps him up, and chats with him a bit: he is married, loves his wife, has three kids—and the fugitive, visibly moved, waits very politely for him to finish before beginning to run again. A "strong" situation in the traditional style has been set up, and then destroyed in the midst of its development by a desire for demystification that uses every possible means to make its way: banality, the greyish humor of everyday or common life, and some not very elegant methods—jokes that are stupid and in bad taste, and inflated stories. The same procedure is used throughout the film and constantly brings into question the dramatic economy which the viewer has risked allowing himself to be taken in by. For example, in David Goodis's work, the two killers are members of an awesome organization; they represent an insidious and terrifying menace which expresses itself through these two shabby characters, who aren't menacing in themselves but in what they represent. Truffaut carefully preserves the ludicrous aspect of the two gangsters, their stupidities, their clumsiness, while at the same time he still accents the demystification of the killer already palpable in Goodis. Truffaut's crooks are more true than life—therefore, they are tinged with unreality. They are not gangsters, but mediocre men playing at being gangsters, and playing poorly. Ludicrous and ineffectual, they barely know how to drive. They are unaware of the ABC's of their trade and are as obsessed with women as schoolboys. They are fond of baroque gadgets (musical cigarette lighters, scarves made out of Japanese metal) and are at ease with no one but the dreadful boy in the film, in whom they find an interlocutor worthy of them. All in all, they would be absolutely inoffensive if they didn't have a pistol that they use more willingly as a calling card—the tangible symbol of their function—than as a weapon.

The detective story background is more effectively undercut by the staging than by the witticisms of the scenario (like the mother who dies because of her son's false oath); with the greatest detachment, the staging presents all the scenes of violence and action with a destructive irony. To make this point I must, of course, cite the final sequence of the grand reckoning, filmed with a long shot in a Christmas-card setting, where the combatants stamp in the snow and exchange badly aimed shots, chasing each other all around the house like kids. The site chosen for the camera, resolutely withdrawn from an action that it seems to film as if by chance, dissociated from it, is exactly the place where Truffaut places himself in relation to the apparent line of his film, to the "plot" he pretends to allow to unfold all by itself (to prevent the viewer from being too concerned with it), so that he can suggest that the essence of what he's doing is always somewhere else, and to invite the viewer to look for it off-screen, and—why not?—outside the film. Now, with this first destructive enterprise carried out so well, you could think about going on and finally penetrating deeper into this secretive work with the certainty of finding the thread of connection. If Truffaut expended all his energy to convince us that *Shoot the Piano Player* isn't a "black" film, we can now expect to discover its true face: the efforts of the director and the spectator will finally be repaid. Meanwhile, a little patience.

SECOND VIEWING

When the new superimposes itself on the old, the French cinema splits under the double weight of false legends. While we wait for the necessary publication of a book about "subrealism" in the cinema, almost entirely devoted to French cinema, with an additional chapter on neo-subrealism, *Shoot the Piano Player* already presents us with a repertoire sufficiently stocked with the characteristic traits of the new school. If Truffaut so effectively resists making a film in the tradition of the "old-time movie," could it be that *Shoot the Piano Player* is a New Wave film? At first everything seems to confirm this hypothesis: from the casualness of the treatment of the scenario to the occasionally fuzzy shots of Raoul Coutard and the encroaching, haunting, and enticing influence of Godard, the hateful details settle in with great authority. The gigantic motorized *Cahiers du Cinéma*, the love scene under the sheets, the disrespectful allusions to the great masters (Gance, Vadim), the barely audible dialogue, the private jokes for little pals, the hustling style of directing—all place the film in too precise a context for it to be argued that Truffaut simply wanted to renounce a contemporary taste that elsewhere he had strongly helped to create. Why not disengage yourself to go take the air of another time, that of Autant-Lara—Truffaut's hearty beast from whom he has taken so much— no one would reproach you for going to pay your visits to the *Bois des Amants*. Well, yes, *Shoot the Piano Player* is precisely placed in 1960, at a moment in French cinema that we have little reason to like. Perhaps the flourishes of the modern style will seem as delectable to future generations as those of the Modern Style are for us. Let us age quickly.

THIRD VIEWING

With *The 400 Blows,* a film shot in the first person, Truffaut gave us (no one is unaware of it) his autobiography, very edifying besides. Since movie criticism is almost a century behind criticism in general—it's had its Sainte-Beuve and is waiting for its Baude-laire—it may seem original to point out that an artist exposes himself with more abandon in an apparently objective work than in pretended intimate journals, which are generally fraudulent. To give an example: there are strong reasons to think that David Lean's *Summertime* is a greater revelation of its director's personality than *Breathless* is of Godard's (to speak of that film again, even by passing over it)—and so much the better or worse for him. I think it's striking to rediscover in certain films this curious mimesis between an actor and his director; to see, for example, at the end of *White Nights* Jean Marais's head resembling Visconti's, to see this ghostly resemblance spread itself over the features of Visconti's actors, to read what Saura said about it to Marcel Oms, and then to see the hero of *Piano Player* incarnated in Aznavour, to think of Truffaut and his biography ground out by publicity—an upward mobility like Vadim's—and to listen to Edouard Saroyan who, on the screen, speaks of the feelings you have when you become rich and famous. And the names of Charlie and Saroyan are not chosen by chance. It's Charlie certainly because Goodis writes that Eddie the piano player looks like Chaplin, and because Charles is the first name of Aznavour, who is so like Saroyan's characters, with their openness and simplicity. That Truffaut enjoys himself and amuses or doesn't amuse us by his quotations, pastiches, or irreverences shouldn't encourage similarly superficial thoughts in us—from "What a sympathetic boy" to "I find him irritating." There is an otherwise serious sequence in *Piano Player,* with an exceptional and at first very obvious gravity of tone, in which Truffaut, taking his distance at the same time that he ingeniously reveals himself, invites us to take our distance, to leave boyishness to the kids (when you've seen one film, you've seen them all), and suddenly sweeps away our reservations. I'm talking about the flashback sequence, carried out with the greatest seriousness, which forms within the film a short film sufficient unto itself and so totally ruptures the tone that, stuck onto the rest like a collage, it profoundly modifies its meaning. Think, for example, of the dream sequence that brightens certain mediocre films; the difference is that in this film, where all conspires to make it unrealistic, this backward glance discovers nothing more than reality itself. The tragically sentimental deception of Edouard Saroyan, betrayed by the woman he loves (and it doesn't matter that it was a good motive, that she betrayed him through devotion) kills Saroyan as surely as if he threw himself out of the window with her as Raymond Rouleau did at the end of Becker's *Falbalas.*

It's all to Truffaut's credit that he dares to shout in 1960, when others shamefacedly invite us to observe the wantonness in the upper class (with a suspicious interest in only the eroticism of the body), that love doesn't work without an absolute demand for fidelity, that the agreement tacitly made between two beings who love each other is so serious that a single betrayal calls for nothing less than death, and a despair worse than death. Edouard Saroyan chooses a more insidious kind of suicide, and perhaps a more efficient one, the *lived* destruction of his personality. After the betrayal and death of his wife—he did nothing to prevent it; he was already detached; and since a woman has betrayed him, what's left but to die?—what can Edouard Saroyan become? The little mechanical piano player of Harriet's Hut? But Charlie has so little existence. He is only the ghost of Saroyan, and the world in which he scarcely lives is beyond reality, beyond the grave, a half-sleep wrapped in cotton (I want to sleep, sleep rather than live . . .).

But this dream refuge is actually a door that opens into nightmare, and it will be enough that a stack of empty boxes collapses for the logic of the dream to open up a series of events all the more frightening because they are a caricature of reality, impossible to question, that you can only submit to like a set of dissolving fantasies. All depersonalization, imaged in the little death of sleep, is accompanied by a radical "derealization" of the external world, and by an oppressive feeling of strangeness, a lack of familiarity with real life. In this subjective upset, born of depressed states, the emotional self relaxes its relationships and breaks all contact with the world around it. But the world continues to exist, to unfold its long chain of derisory events, until the death of a young girl, who ought to have been loved. Charlie must let her die without being able to prevent it (or wishing to) because he is outside the world, an accursed being who can cause only the unhappiness of those who get close to him. *Shoot the Piano Player* bears witness to the impossibility and horror of living on the sidelines. This is an apparently detached film, overwhelming in one's first viewing of its shame and morbid timidity (because isn't timidity here the symptom of a secret culpability?), that nevertheless confesses everything. It is a neurotic work, which multiplies the detours and recesses of repression, yet in which the triumphant obsession finally comes out. You have to be singularly gifted, or similarly obsessed, to follow the unconscious drama of the piano player's libido from your first sight of him. But once you find the thread, everything becomes clear, even the obscurities, hesitations, failures, and self-destruction of a work that presents itself with all the disturbing evidence and discomfort of a stillborn action.

First the anguish, the fear of living. After twenty admirable reverse angle shots (the faces in close-up of Plyne and Charlie), fear appears in Aznavour's face. "It's true, I'm afraid . . . I'm afraid . . ." A fear of the world, already perceptible in the famous interview [with the psychiatrist] in *The 400 Blows*; a desire to see things coupled with an impotency to attain them; a false lucidity; and especially a fear of women, a fear of everything the other sex has of the mysterious, the foreigner, and the enemy. Here Aznavour's popular character is invoked like a quotation, his "sexual obsessions" that have been popularized by songs that Truffaut (it's said) scarcely appreciates, although many sequences would suggest a musical commentary where the "fans" will recognize in passing *Ce sacré piano* and *Après l'amour* obviously, but also *Comme des étrangers* and *Mon amour protège-moi*. The atmosphere of Aznavour's songs, so close to that of the film, contributes still more to make this privileged actor into the twin and brother of Truffaut. But in different degrees all the characters carry within them this

Baudelairian obsession with Woman, and all are brothers in this morbid impotency to understand her, to understand the movers of this disconcerting merry-go-round, the meaning of this existence.

As fundamental and sordid as the reflections of the two killers seem, they make us think. Why do women have naked legs under their dressing gowns? Why do their uncovered legs disturb us so much? The whole scene in the car intrigues the viewer, because he is worried about avoiding his own embarrassment in order to find out where it ends: the beautiful and mysterious smile that plays over Marie Dubois's lips when Charlie says: "When you know one woman, you know them all" (a very revealing phrase for an analyst), the girl's great burst of laughter, the worried looks of the hooligans. Do we have to look too hard for this kind of thought in the most unexpected character, Plyne, in the astonishing sequence of his death? Isn't the troubling nostalgia for women he expresses the same as Charlie's before his wife's betrayal? Isn't it also the nostalgia of François Truffaut, in spite of and perhaps because of the extreme derision with which he emphasizes it? The waitress has just attacked Plyne in particularly insulting terms. He has been in love with her for a long time, in "romantic" love. She is the image of the ideal woman for him. He doesn't understand. "Such gross words in such a pretty mouth. She's not a real woman. She isn't a Woman. Woman is pure, Woman is sublime, Woman is a magical being."

At this moment Plyne's voice strangely resembles the voice at the end of Preminger's *Laura* that proclaims from the radio both the impossibility and the absolute necessity of love. Even when certain words are tainted by a modern derision, it is comforting that they be resaid, that a certain sensibility that one has thought lost forever could be dimly retrieved. Of course, it can't be denied that the fringe of uncertainty and confusion that obscures Truffaut's film reduces this interpretation to a kind of light-headed criticism. Yet it is rare in our time that a film can still make us dream. Why should we refuse this pleasure while we wait for the reinvention of a cinema that we used to love, a cinema that doesn't have to be "modern," so long as it again finds the roads of the heart.

SHOOT THE PIANO PLAYER
by PAULINE KAEL

The cover of David Goodis's novel *Down There,* now issued by Grove Press under the title of the film adapted from it, *Shoot the Piano Player,* carries a statement from Henry Miller—"Truffaut's film was so good I had doubts the book could equal it. I have just read the novel and I think it is even better than the film." I don't agree with Miller's judgment. I like the David Goodis book, but it's strictly a work in a limited genre, well-done and consistent; Truffaut's film busts out all over—and that's what's wonderful about it. The film is comedy, pathos, tragedy all scrambled up— much I think as most of us really experience them (surely all our lives are filled with comic horrors) but not as we have been led to expect them in films.

Shoot the Piano Player is about a man who has withdrawn from human experience; he wants not to care any more, not to get involved, not to *feel.* He has reduced life to a level on which he can cope with it—a reverie between him and the piano. Everything that happens outside his solitary life seems erratic, accidental, unpredictable—but he can predict the pain. In a flashback we see why: when he *did* care, he failed the wife who needed him and caused her death. In the course of the film he is once more brought back into the arena of human contacts; another girl is destroyed, and he withdraws again into solitude.

Truffaut is a free and inventive director—and he fills the piano player's encounters with the world with good and bad jokes, bits from old Sacha Guitry films, clowns and thugs, tough kids, songs and fantasy and snow scenes, and homage to the American gangster films—not the classics, the socially conscious big-studio gangster films of the thirties, but the grade-B gangster films of the forties and fifties. Like Godard, who dedicated *Breathless* to Monogram Pictures, Truffaut is young, and he loves the cheap American gangster films of his childhood and youth. And like them, *Shoot the Piano Player* was made on a small budget. It was also made outside of studios with a crew that, according to witnesses, sometimes consisted of Truffaut, the actors, and a cameraman. Part of his love of cheap American movies with their dream imagery of the American gangster—the modern fairy tales for European children who go to movies—is no doubt reflected in his taking an American underworld novel and transferring its setting from Philadelphia to France.

Charles Aznavour who plays the hero is a popular singer turned actor—rather like Frank Sinatra in this country, and like Sinatra, he is an instinctive actor and a great camera subject. Aznavour's piano player is like a tragic embodiment of Robert Hutchins's Zukerkandl philosophy (whatever it is, stay out of it): he is the thinnest-skinned of modern heroes. It is his own capacity to feel that makes him cut himself off: he experiences so sensitively and so acutely that he can't bear the suffering of it—he thinks that if he doesn't do anything he won't feel and he won't cause suffering to others. The girl, Marie Dubois—later the smoky-steam-engine girl of *Jules and Jim*—is like a Hollywood forties movie type; she would have played well with Humphrey Bogart—a big, clear-eyed, crude, loyal, honest girl. The film is closely related to Godard's *Breathless*; and both seem to be haunted by the shade of Bogart.

Shoot the Piano Player is both nihilistic in attitude and, at the same time, in its wit and good spirits, totally involved in life and fun. Whatever Truffaut touches seems to leap to life—even a gangster thriller is transformed into the human comedy. A *comedy* about melancholia, about the hopelessness of life can only give the lie to the theme; for as long as we can joke, life is not hopeless; we can enjoy it. In Truffaut's style there is so much pleasure in life that the wry, lonely little piano player, the sardonic little man who shrugs off experience, is himself a beautiful character. This beauty is a tribute to human experience, even if the man is so hurt and defeated that he can only negate experience. The nihilism of the character—and the anarchic nihilism of the director's style—have led reviewers to call the film a surrealist farce; it isn't that strange.

When I refer to Truffaut's style as anarchic and nihilistic, I am referring to a *style,* not an absence of it. I disagree with the critics around the country who find the film disorganized; they seem to cling to the critical apparatus of their grammar school teachers. They want unity of theme, easy-to-follow-transitions in mood, a good, coherent, old-fashioned plot, and heroes they can identify with and villains they can reject. Stanley Kauffmann in the *New Republic* compares *Shoot the Piano Player* with the sweepings of cutting room floors; *Time* decides that "the moral, if any, seems to be that shooting the piano player might, at least, put the poor devil out of his misery." But who but *Time* is looking for a moral? What's exciting about movies like *Shoot The Piano Player, Breathless* (and also the superb *Jules and Jim,* though it's very different from the other two) is that they, quite literally, move with the times. They are full of unresolved, inexplicable, disharmonious elements, irony and slapstick and defeat all compounded—*not* arbitrarily as the reviewers claim—but in terms of the filmmaker's efforts to find some expression for his own anarchic experience, instead of making more of those tiresome well-made movies that no longer mean much to us.

The subject matter of *Shoot the Piano Player,* as of *Breathless,* seems small and unimportant compared to the big themes of so many films, but it only *seems* small: it is an effort to deal with contemporary experience in terms drawn out of that experience. For both Godard and Truffaut a good part of this experience has been moviegoing, but this is just as much a part of their lives as reading is for a writer. And what writer does not draw upon what he has read?

A number of reviewers have complained that in his improvisatory method, Truffaut includes irrelevancies, and they use as chief illustration the opening scene—a gangster who is running away from pursuers bangs into a lamppost, and then is helped to his feet by a man who proceeds to walk along with him, while discussing his marital life. Is it really so irrelevant? Only if you grew up in that tradition of the well-made play in which this bystander would have to reappear as some vital link in the plot. But he's relevant in a different way here: he helps to set us in a world in which his seminormal existence seems just as much a matter of chance and fringe behavior and simplicity as the gangster's existence—which begins to seem seminormal also. The bystander talks; we get an impression of his way of life and his need to talk about it, and he goes out of the film, and that is that: Truffaut would have to be as stodgy and dull witted as the reviewers to bring him back and link him into the story. For the meaning of these films is that these fortuitous encounters illuminate something about our lives in a way that the old neat plots don't.

There is a tension in the method; we never quite know where we are, how we are supposed to react—and this tension, as the moods change and we are pulled in different ways, gives us the excitement of drama, of art, of *our* life. Nothing is clear-cut, the ironies crisscross and bounce. The loyal, courageous heroine is so determined to live by her code that when it's violated, she comes on too strong, and the piano player is repelled by her inability to respect the weaknesses of others. Thugs kidnapping a little boy discuss their possessions with him—a conversation worthy of a footnote in Veblen's passages on conspicuous expenditure.

Only a really carefree, sophisticated filmmaker could bring it off —and satisfy our desire for the unexpected that is also *right*. Truffaut is a director of incredible taste; he never carries a scene *too* far. It seems extraordinarily simple to complain that a virtuoso who can combine many moods has not stuck to one familiar old mood—but this is what the reviews seem to amount to. The modern novel has abandoned the old conception that each piece must be in place—abandoned it so thoroughly that when we read something like Angus Wilson's *Anglo-Saxon Attitudes* in which each piece does finally fit in place, we are astonished and amused at the dexterity of the accomplishment. That is the way Wilson works and it's wonderfully satisfying, but few modern novelists work that way; and it would be as irrelevant to the meaning and quality of, say, *Tropic of Capricorn* to complain that the plot isn't neatly tied together like *Great Expectations,* as to complain of the film *Shoot the Piano Player* that it isn't neatly tied together like *The Bicycle Thief.* Dwight Macdonald wrote that *Shoot the Piano Player* deliberately mixed up "three genres which are usually kept apart: crime melodrama, romance, and slapstick comedy." And, he says, "I thought the mixture didn't jell, but it was an exhilarating try." What I think is exhilarating in *Shoot the Piano Player* is that it *doesn't* "jell" and that the different elements keep *us* in a state of suspension—we react far more than we do to works that "jell." Incidentally, it's not completely accurate to say that these genres are usually kept apart; although *slapstick* rarely enters the mixture except in a far-out film like *Beat the Devil* or *Lovers and Thieves* or the new *The Manchurian Candidate,* there are numerous examples of crime melodrama-romance-comedy among well-known American films—particularly of the forties—for example *The Maltese Falcon, Casablanca, The Big Sleep, To Have and Have Not.* (Not all of Truffaut's models are cheap B-pictures.)

Perhaps one of the problems that American critics and audiences may have with *Shoot the Piano Player* is a peculiarly American element in it—the romantic treatment of the man who walks alone. For decades our films were full of these gangsters, outcasts, detectives, cynics; Bogart epitomized them all—all the men who had been hurt by a woman or betrayed by their friends and who no longer trusted anybody. And although I think most of us enjoyed this romantic treatment of the man beyond the law, we rejected it intellectually. It was part of hack moviemaking—we might love it but it wasn't really intellectually respectable. And now here it is, inspired by our movies, and coming back to us via France. The heroine of *Shoot the Piano Player* says of the hero, "Even when he's with somebody, he walks alone." But this French hero carries his isolation much farther than the earlier American hero: when his girl is having a fight on his behalf and he is impelled to intervene, he says to himself, "You're out of it. Let them fight it out." He is brought into it; but where the American hero, once impelled to move, is a changed man and, redeemed by love or patriotism or a sense of fair play, he would take the initiative, save his girl, and conquer everything, this French hero simply moves into the situation when he must, when he can no longer stay out of it, and takes the consequences. He finds that the contact with people is once again defeating. He really doesn't believe in anything; the American hero only *pretended* he didn't.

Breathless was about active, thoughtless young people; *Shoot the Piano Player* is about a passive, melancholic character who is acted upon. Yet the world that surrounds the principal figures in these two movies is similar: the clowns in one are police, in the other gangsters, but this hardly matters. What we react to in both is the world of absurdities that is so much like our own world in which people suddenly and unexpectedly turn into clowns. But at the center is the sentimentalist—Belmondo in *Breathless,* Aznavour here —and I think there can be no doubt that both Godard and Truffaut love their heroes.

There are incidentally a number of little in-group jokes included in the film; a few of these are of sufficiently general interest to be worth mentioning, and, according to Andrew Sarris, they have been verified by Truffaut. The piano player is given the name of Saroyan as a tribute to William Saroyan, particularly for his volume of stories *The Man on the Flying Trapeze,* and also because Charles Aznavour, like Saroyan, is Armenian (and, I would surmise, for the playful irony of giving a life-evading hero the name of one of the most rambunctious of life-embracing writers). One of the hero's brothers in the film is named Chico, as a tribute to the Marx Brothers. And the impresario in the film, the major villain of the work, is called Lars Schmeel, as a disapproving gesture toward someone Truffaut does *not* admire—the impresario Lars Schmidt, known to us simply as Ingrid Bergman's current husband, but apparently known to others—and disliked by Truffaut—for his theatrical activities in Paris.

If a more pretentious vocabulary or a philosophic explanation will help, the piano player is intensely human and sympathetic, a character who empathizes with others, and with whom we, as audience, empathize; but he does not want to accept the responsibilities of his humanity—he asks only to be left alone. And because he refuses voluntary involvement, he is at the mercy of accidental forces. He is, finally, man trying to preserve his little bit of humanity in a chaotic world—it is not merely a world he never made but a world he would much rather forget about. But schizophrenia cannot be willed and so long as he is sane, he is only partly successful: crazy accidents happen—and sometimes he must deal with them. That is to say, no matter how far he retreats from life, he is not completely safe. And Truffaut himself is so completely engaged in life that he pleads for the piano player's right to be left alone, to live in his withdrawn state, *to be out of it*. Truffaut's plea is, of course, "Don't shoot the piano player."

François Truffaut
—The Anarchist Imagination
by JUDITH SHATNOFF

The problem is: a phenomenal young talent which gives no quarter and demands the ultimate in tolerance.

One can either submit with a helpless bow, or retreat to the more comfortable artistry of a fashionable crew—the Fellinis, Viscontis, Bergmans, Resnais—or rush even farther backward to the primitive security of Hollywood cinema chiefs who show a chair as a chair as a chair.

For the braver critics there is François Truffaut, who has come to the screen in a whirlwind of amoral energy. Whether we like what he does or not, he can't be ignored. He's a dangerous talent.

To begin with, he's dangerous because of his sense of form, which is highly personal, subject to quirks and shifts. And he's dangerous because his use of time upsets what we've come to expect from recent film art: either a delicate rendering of fractured moments (Kurosawa, Resnais), or a brutal re-creation of a minute as a minute (Antonioni). And Truffaut is dangerous because he specializes in weird combinations: tragedy plus comedy plus melodrama plus slapstick; and because he's able to balance these combinations so tastefully they "work." But mostly, he is dangerous because he continually thinks.

He thinks on a visual level:

From Film Quarterly *16, no. 3 (Spring 1963): 3–11. Copyright ©
1963 by the Regents of the University of California. Reprinted by permission of the author and the Regents.*

Odd camera angles, high-key exposures, grain, interspersed stop-and-go motion, sequences which suddenly zoom into a bird's eye view, multiple-scene frame, cutouts, squares of action surrounded by black—Truffaut uses whatever technique suits his purpose, or his whim. He will shorten or lengthen scenes for an effect, for a change of pace, for a joke, for their beauty. Consider, for instance, the race in the early part of *Jules and Jim*. It was run to show that Catherine will break any rules to win, but it was photographed in blurs and close-ups which are rhythmical studies of motion, reminiscent of Kurosawa's treatment of horseback riders in *Throne of Blood*. In *Shoot the Piano Player*, overlapped stopped views of lovers asleep in bed are used to show passage of time; but they also create a high-key montage of bodies, scattered clothing, and objects, which is abstractly beautiful. The scenes of the boy in *The 400 Blows* spinning in an amusement park centrifuge are mainly included for visual dazzle. But above all—whether initiated by whim or reason —the camera technique and the audacious editing (especially in the opening ten minutes of *Jules and Jim*) are the work of an artist who knows exactly what he is doing and does not for a moment give up or lose control.

Some devotees would say the same for *Last Year at Marienbad;* but *Marienbad* is all visual icing, as elegant and as blatantly mannered as the plaster curlicues in the tiny summerhouse of Nymphenbeg Palace which Resnais photographed up, down, and sideways in his opening sequence. In tone, *Marienbad* is equivalent to a fugue based on "Three Blind Mice," and its content is no more worth unraveling than a puns and anagrams crossword puzzle. François Truffaut, in his three major films, gives us as much visual dash and splendor as we can possibly admire, but in addition his cinematic virtuosity expresses a complex and dangerous point of view. He is the equal of Michaelangelo Antonioni—with one important difference. Antonioni bravely leads us through despair to the blank wall of meaninglessness only to stop short before the rear exit—the exciting circuit to pleasure, absurd joy—supplied by the best existential thinkers, everyone from Albert Camus to Paul Tillich. Truffaut doesn't stop short. He's an ex-j.d., a slum kid with a slum kid's energy and ability to thumb his nose and laugh and suffer simultaneously. He's also a French intellectual—a special breed

nurtured over centuries to despise sentimentality. All these qualities
are present in his three feature-length films, and they supply the
dramatic tension of high art.

It's at first hard to understand *The 400 Blows* in relation to
Truffaut's later work, for in some ways it isn't a French film at all,
but an excellent version of the American "art" movie. What is remarkable about these movies is their lack of philosophical base.
They spring, instead, from an adolescent verve (*Shadows, Senseless,*
or any "experimental" film you can name), and rapidly fizz out; or
they lean heavily on The Problem motif in amateur sociology (*The
Defiant Ones, Come Back, Little Sheba, The Connection,* etc.); or
they sell a version of Freud which even the vulgar can applaud
(see, for example, the ecstatic reviews in *Time* of *David and Lisa,*
a psychiatric soap opera which drags and lisps out the "truths" of
The Snake Pit (1946) and *Spellbound* (1945) as if they were tomorrow's revelations).

The 400 Blows has many memorable scenes, including some which
allude to Jean Vigo's *Zéro de Conduite.* The boy and his stepfather
happily cooking together in their miserable little kitchen, an inane
interview with an off-screen psychologist, the boy enjoying a rare
outing with his mother and stepfather, the running views of Paris
through the grille of a police wagon, are fine. But now and then,
despite the autobiographical "necessity" which gives *The 400 Blows*
its force, it's preachy. It levels an accusing finger at "you out there"
—society—following the best of Stanley Kramer gestures.

True, French law is brutal and perverse: a man is guilty until he
proves himself innocent; a man can be held incommunicado for
days in one of those clever chicken-cages, shown in the film, in
which young, old, murderers, maniacs, pickpockets, traffic violators,
are thrown together indiscriminately. James Baldwin, in an essay,
described how he was caught in Paris with a stolen bedsheet in his
possession (innocently so), and subjected to the medieval niceties
of the French criminal code. Baldwin, an adult American, finally
got help from outside. Truffaut himself was rescued from a prison
sentence by the famous critic André Bazin, whose protegé he became. But no such luck for the boy-hero of *The 400 Blows.* He is a
straw tossed by twin hurricanes: his family and society. His crime

is trivial; his capture is ironic. The treatment he receives is heart-less and unreasonable. It suggests that a society which has always prided itself on its rational base is really inhuman; that to fear this society is not paranoiac, but logical and necessary. And when the boy escapes from a reformatory and runs for the ocean, merely to see it for the first time, his action is far more respectable than the rigid social structure which has battered him about. It is here, at the end of the film, when the boy stands in the surf, that Truffaut makes the comment which goes beyond any of those sociological clichés we are too often asked to swallow as important messages.

Here Truffaut's "thinking" shows. For we have identified with the underdog as incident upon incident piles against him; we can't help but cheer his run for freedom. And suddenly, we are stopped; the boy stops, sociology stops, the film stops. What now? Where next? The poor dreamer has run to and *through* his dream. Mis-treatment and misunderstanding fuse as we are asked to consider something shocking: If the reality of our dreams is as futile as the reality of experience, what is left? Where can one run? The ques-tion remains as motion stops and a grainy image of the boy as a clipped newspaper photo, dehumanized, hangs on the screen.

It is from this ironic position, this inquiry into absurdity, that *Shoot the Piano Player* begins; and fiercely, wildly, it pushes beyond any adolescent or Beat glee in the destruction of form and symbol to a resolution which is as effective as a blow on the head. It's a fascinating accomplishment. It works through an exploitation of incongruity, and we, the audience, are its happy victims.

The opening sequence of *Shoot the Piano Player* is characteristic. A man runs desperately through the foggy dark streets of Paris. We can see the strain on his face and hear the panting of his breath above the urgent clatter of his heels, and from long experience we know what all that means. Then he collides, comically, with a lamp-post. He moans, he groans, he rubs his head, and a hand reaches for him. He's caught! Yes? No. He's helped to his feet by a com-placent passerby, and the two walk on casually, joking, and dis-cussing the pros and cons of marriage. This chit-chat is allowed to continue long enough to assuage any sensation of desperation or danger which may have been left over from the opening scene, and,

1. Charlie Kohler (Charles Aznavour) the piano player.

2. Edouard Saroyan the pianist.

3. Edouard Saroyan playing the "waitress-customer" game with his wife (Nicole Berger).

4. Charlie Kohler wondering whether or not to talk to Léna the waitress (Marie Dubois).

5. Charlie and Léna in bed under Edouard's poster.

6. Léna arguing with Plyne (Serge Davri) while Charlie watches.

7. Charlie and Plyne fighting after Plyne has his Léna.

8. "Charlie, old buddy, let me be familiar, Charlie, old buddy, you're going to die."

9. Ernest (Daniel Boulanger) and Momo (Claude Mansard),
the gangsters.

10. Production shot: the hideaway, Truffaut walking between
Richard Kanayan (Fido) and Marie Dubois.

11. Production shot: Truffaut showing Charles Aznavour where he wants Marie Dubois to lie for her death scene.

as soon as this is gauged to have been accomplished, our man runs off even more desperately in another direction. He is still being chased; his life is still in danger; and we sit gaping in surprise.

Our next view of him is when he enters a cabaret, greets his brother "Charlie" Saroyan, the piano player, and talks vaguely of his troubles. When Charlie refuses help, the desperate runner simply begins to enjoy himself dancing with the local whores. Once again we are surprised. Surely no man in danger would dance with such abandon at such a time. We are further misled by a scene which raises *Shoot the Piano Player* to high comedy. A waiter gets up onto the bandstand to sing. He is shot head-on, from a fixed camera position, as he sways and bounces up and down, deadpan, singing verse after verse of what must be the wittiest song yet heard in films: the blight on the berry (a euphemism for an unlucky lady). While we are still laughing, the pursuing gangsters catch up with our "desperate" man. And it is no joke. They carry loaded revolvers. Once more a desperate chase begins and we wonder: where are we? in comedy? In the shock of ironic juxtapositions?

This is clearly indicated in the long flashback which tells the history of the piano player. Only in this sequence does Truffaut use a standard, chronological presentation which leaves us in no doubt which attitude to adopt. It's a tragic story with cynical overtones: a talented pianist gets his first concert opportunity because his wife sleeps with an impresario. In itself this is nothing unusual; we're all cynically aware that a roll in the hay has been the start of many brilliant careers. But it proves tragic for the pianist and his wife, for she commits suicide during the moment he flees from her.

In one moment, through one act, everything which took years— a lifetime—to accomplish becomes meaningless; perhaps it always was meaningless. The pianist turns his back on success, on ambition, on effort, on feeling. He can't exorcise his love of music, but he can refuse to do anything more than just play the piano. In a world which can suddenly become meaningless, why should anything be done with or about anything? Thus, Charlie barely responds to his new girl's ambitious proposal to reinstate him as a serious artist. He smiles vaguely and lets her do as she likes. Unfortunately, she is vulgar and gets him into trouble. Later, oddly, she is killed. Why? Well, why does anything happen? Because it does. If there is any unifying tone in the film it is an existential irrelevance, coupled with a shrug from Charles Aznavour, a masterful actor, which asks, What did you expect? Existence is a succession of dirty jokes: nothing lasts, struggle is futile, hope is obscene. (The title *Shoot the Piano Player* refers to a barroom sign in old Westerns —"Don't Shoot the Piano Player"—but Truffaut's film might as easily be called *Why Not Shoot the Piano Player?*)

Ironic juxtapositions are used on another, equally deadly, level through the gangsters who kidnap Charlie and his girl. Never did two gangsters behave more like businessmen suffering from indigestion. All the ominous old gangster conventions from Al Capone to *Rififi* have been blithely avoided for the gangster unconventions of farce, such as the ones which open the hilarious movie, *Some Like It Hot.* At one point, after one gangster swears he is telling the truth or may his mother drop dead, there is a flash shot of a skinny old woman kicking up her heels and dropping dead. The slapstick is a little forced, but funny. Then our hero and heroine make a nonchalant escape. Yes, this is farce; we feel assured. Thus, towards the end, when these same lovable gangsters behave ruthlessly, when real bullets scatter and someone is actually, senselessly killed, we are as shocked as if a gentle neighbor suddenly ran berserk with an ax.

What has occurred throughout *Shoot the Piano Player* is the deliberate explosion of each cliché in turn, or, to be more precise, a deliberate destruction of the expected order of events. A series of clues which usually lead in one direction are abruptly, deliberately, interrupted and rushed in another direction. On-track, off-track, on a new track, off that, we in the audience are shunted around until we give up and docilely obey Truffaut, the ringmaster. Our judgment has proven wrong so many times, at last we sit with judgment suspended, forced outside logic into a hodgepodge of pain and pleasure. A mock fight between the piano player and his boss can turn deadly serious. A young girl can be killed by a stray bullet and her headlong slide down a snowy slope can be breathtakingly beautiful. A good man can produce evil as easily as an evil man. In fact, there is no such thing as good *or* evil; there are only complex mixtures of both, and there is circumstance. There is also a muddled reference to fate or blood-curse in the talk among Charlie and his brothers; but the real explanation is that there is no explanation. Life is unpredictable and inexplicable. It simply happens. There are lulls in the process of destruction, some fun, some love, some success; but finally, we are left with a tinkling, mocking little tune. Truffaut has managed to do what Henry Miller always tries to do: disrupt, disorientate, kiss You, spit in Your eye.[1]

Jules and Jim does the same in a more sophisticated style. Here, Truffaut isn't as autocratic in his method of control, but wins his way through charm, wheedling and coaxing the viewer to give up his standard of judgment—especially his moral standard—and his usual pattern of perception and interpretation.

At first this is accomplished by a quick series of whimsical, charming views of the exploits of Jules and Jim, Mutt and Jeff, Sancho Panza and Don Quixote (as they prefer to call themselves, thereby ennobling their comic aspects), a gangly, effervescent pair of innocent libertines looking for someone to worship—Dulcinea, perhaps? They find her, first as a statue, then in the flesh: Catherine, who, if we are to trust those dear boys, Jules and Jim, is the quintessence of female charm.

Charm is the key to the film. In *Une Histoire d'Eau,* a short Truffaut made with Jean-Luc Godard in 1958, the touch of irreverent charm was already apparent. An ultra-Gallic pair enjoy the flooding of a river: they race a car along a flooded road, spraying the drowned countryside with their gay wash; they jitterbug on the one square of dry land left; they picnic and make impossibly French faces at each other. Death, inconvenience, millions of dollars of damage may have resulted from this flood, but we are never told about it; it's simply an occasion for charming fun. It also shows Truffaut's rare joyous quality—one that is much less fashionable and much more difficult to express than Swedish gloom or Italian emptiness.

Jules and Jim is a literate film. It is based on a novel (as is *Shoot*

---

[1] Perhaps Truffaut succeeds because a film can control both the visual and auditory perceptions of its audience, whereas a novel can only approximate a visual world through imagery, and must, therefore, rely on its energy to construct its "closed universe." Perhaps in this sense the film is more dangerous and potentially greater than the novel as an art form.

the Piano Player) and there are references to literature throughout, such as the continual mention of Cervantes's pair of heroes. Jules and Jim, both writers, are part of a bohemian circle of artists, and a newsclip of Nazi book-burning implies the barbarism which ended that post-World War I intellectual and artistic period in Europe. There is even a famous literary precedent for their maison à trois, Voltaire's fifteen-year affair with Mme. du Châtelet—although Voltaire and the Marquis du Châtelet were not as close friends originally as Jules and Jim.

Visually, the film echoes Jean Renoir, and no film since *A Day in the Country* has been as charming as *Jules and Jim*. It is delicately lighted; its historical atmosphere is effortlessly correct. There is only beauty in the landscapes, the architecture, the faces, the gestures, the period costumes—and for a reason: the visual loveliness contributes to the idyllic misrepresentation. It's a deft seduction. It prepares us to accept whatever unorthodoxy appears on screen, until any bluster of "Thou shalt not . . ." as a reaction to Catherine's behavior becomes irrelevant. Once again judgment is suspended—not through shock as in *Shoot the Piano Player*—but pleasantly. We are won to acceptance through beauty and spontaneity, and there we are for a while, poignantly wondering at ourselves re-created as we never were.

For Jules, Jim, and Catherine are children, just the sort of children we would have grown up to be if the nasty real world hadn't interfered. Jules and Jim are the sweet children and Catherine is the bad child, the mischievous demigod who makes life fascinating but exacts payment in absolute loyalty. The nasty real world finally intrudes in the form of rough newsclips of World War I, but it does little to mature our boys. It makes them a little sadder than before, and it makes them need someone to worship even more.

True, they are beginning to despair of human love. Jules remarks that someday he will write a love story and all the characters will be insects. But they are firm in their adoration of Catherine—almost as firm as she is in demanding it.

The price is high but so are the rewards, for Jeanne Moreau's portrayal of Catherine is brilliantly charming. She is charming when she makes funny faces, cuddles in bed, sings songs, rides a bicycle, skips stones, and especially charming when she plays tag. "Catch me," she says, tapping Jim on the shoulder and galloping off; she is thirty-two and looks older—a genius stroke of casting, for a baby-faced Catherine would be banal. She invents a charming game called The Village Idiot to amuse her adorers. Oskar Werner, Henri Serre, Jeanne Moreau, and a Jane Withers midget-type of child (an awful choice, whether deliberate or accidental) sit gibbering and twisting their faces at each other as the picture spins and reels round and round like a child spinning and reeling with delight. It's a pure re-creation of youthful joy. We can identify wholeheartedly with our carefree friends, who hardly ever remember they are adults with the weary weight of adult responsibility ready to fall on them at any moment. Truffaut doesn't moralize, and why should we? We are enjoying an emotion which hasn't been as splendidly re-created on the screen since the swinging, giggling expression of young love in *Miracle in Milan*. To judge our friends in any way is to impose external standards on their "world."

Similarly, to interpret Catherine's jump into the Seine as her "act of freedom" goes beyond the limits of the film, for the jump is only free as an act of childish derring-do is free. It fits with the behavior of the two children in the British thriller *The Yellow Balloon* who tragically dare each other to jump the chasms between bomb ruins. It's no "proof" that women are more equal than men, at least more courageous about jumping into rivers, and wasn't meant to be. Truffaut would never be so provincial as to show Catherine hooting and tooting feminist propaganda. He simply shows her: here she is. Here is her gang.

What the jump does prove is that Jules and Jim are ninnies, that Catherine knows it, and that she has chosen them precisely for their perfectly charming ninnyness.

As the boys walk along the banks of the Seine they blabber nonsense about the inferiority of women. When Jules reaches the final silliness—a woman would never be allowed in the presence of God —Catherine orders Jim to protest. "I protest," he says weakly, after a moment, and she jumps, because her subject's performance hasn't been good enough. Stop that blabbering and look at me, her jump orders; I am I and I am better than you and don't you forget it! Her jump is an act of arrogance and egotism. It's an act of passion, and for that reason, despite everything which follows, Catherine is great. We must honor her intensity at the essence of greatness; she adds magic to a story of two sweet ninnies.

But Catherine's is a vastly limited force and shouldn't be mistaken for freedom. Her passions are great, but she is their victim. They control her. She isn't free. And anyway, *Jules and Jim* isn't about freedom; it's about fantasy. It is fantasy.

More pertinent than the jump to understanding the film is the story Jim tells Jules and Albert about the French soldier who wrote letters to a casual lady friend every night in the trenches. At first these letters were formal, then they became more and more loving, then passionate, until an engagement was proposed and marriage arranged. But two days before the Armistice, before passion by correspondence could be consummated, the soldier was killed. As Jim explains it, such an extraordinary affair could never have developed without the stimulating danger of death in war. His friends agree and sit silently gazing at the magnificent scenery. They can all appreciate how lucky a man is to have his fantasy forever protected as fantasy. Death has preserved what life would inevitably destroy. It's sad, but they savor the paradox, sigh, and rush off after their common dangerous fantasy: Catherine.

The parallels are obvious. The story Jim tells is the example which precedes the example of a major fantasy acted out to its conclusion. And, in terms of an adult world, the child's conclusion must be destructive.

Thus, Catherine kills herself and Jim. As she drives off the bridge she smiles twice, most charmingly. We watch the car plunge into the river and see bubbles rise to the surface. But it is unbelievable for it is all so charming; the view is so pretty. Therefore, we are shown the cremation of the bodies in rather factual, if uneasy, detail, and the entombment of the ashes. Now we believe. Now we understand Jules's feeling of relief. The great fantasy will be preserved by death, but in life it is done—or is it? What is that charming music which accompanies Jules as he walks stiff-leggedly through the cemetery? We wonder as we realize that Truffaut has succeeded again—this time much more subtly—in being outrageous. Once again he has played, we have danced, and we are left to wipe our kissed and insulted eyes. But we are no longer in a schoolboy-shocker nihilistic mode. We have, instead, approached the anarchical position of the rebel in Camus's terms. We have experienced "an unrepentant work of art."

Many of us have lost sympathy en route. Many may feel that Truffaut's evocation of charm and suspension of judgment hasn't been total enough to make them accept the cruelty which builds and dominates the end of the film—the indiscriminate bed-hopping, betrayal, suicide, murder. It's difficult to be appreciative unless we remember we are not dealing here with life seen through a camera keyhole, but with art. To quote Camus (*The Rebel*):

"Here we have an imaginary world . . . which is created by the rectification of the actual world—a world where suffering can, if it wishes, continue until death, where passions are never distracted, where people are prey to obsessions and are always present to one another. Man is finally able to give himself the alleviating form and limits which he pursues in vain in his own life . . . Far from being moral or purely formal, this alteration aims, primarily, at unity and thereby expresses a metaphysical need . . . On this level [a work of art] is primarily an exercise of intelligence in the service of nostalgic or rebellious sensibilities."

Needless to say, this position is the antithesis of Realism.

Well, we are used to nonrealistic films. We are sophisticated about abstract, surrealist, Dada, Beat films. We are even more sophisticated about the unrealistic commercial movies made in Hollywood about the glamorous life of the working girl, the doctor, the white hunter, the adman, the gunman, the salesman, anybody. We have Stan Brakhage, Walt Disney, *Naked Lunch*, self-destroying machines, and we are comfortable without realism. But we are not comfortable with Truffaut, simply because he refuses to allow it. As soon as we settle down with one metaphor he jars us out and into another, perhaps one which is contradictory. As soon as we pin him down aesthetically, he shrugs us off. Before we can get soulful about the philosophic implications on screen, he makes us laugh. He literally "assaults the sensibilities" in any way he can, using any handy means. Thus, Truffaut, to whom the labels "realism" or "nonrealism" are most likely meaningless, nonetheless deftly and deliberately uses materials of both:

Characters are recognizable, some even empathic, but they develop so complexly shaded, good and bad, strong and weak, that our impression of them, and therefore our identification with them, must be continually revised. Michel, the "hero" of *Breathless* (based on a Truffaut story suggestion) is a prime example of this appealing-repelling mixture; Catherine is another. Settings are accurate to the last detail, but occasionally, deliberately, they are photographed in a way which shatters and rearranges their appearance. Scenes move in climatic order, but in logical disorder, erratically, as life moves; and their is no reason why some episodes follow rather than precede others. Stories hint of important ideas, but there are no "messages" of any kind, anywhere, to clutch and carry off. Most uncomfortable of all, Truffaut doesn't indicate that his realism is or isn't real. He doesn't use any of the paraphernalia of Cocteau, for example, to announce: Attention, this is Art you're watching—Art, not life. And so as an audience we are in the grip of a double irony. There is no safety.

Truffaut does as he pleases. He has an uncanny ability to sense the moment at which to jar us, and enough artistic courage to act swiftly, even violently, to take advantage of that moment. His attitude is iconoclastic—nothing is sacred. It is anarchistic because it is entirely personal, yet tightly controlled; his intellectual vision controls an emotional context for a creative—*not* a destructive or nihilistic—purpose. Truffaut seems to be an anarchist even in relation to his own creations, for he recognizes no structure beyond the one required for each individual work of art, and this, too, is made to be remade. All positions are established to be transcended. All that is constant is the creator himself, saying *Sic volo, sic jubeo* —This I will, this I command. And that, necessarily, is the final statement of great art.

Aznavour Gives the Tone
by FRANÇOIS TRUFFAUT

It was while I was watching *La Tête contre les murs,* Georges
Franju's most beautiful film, that I was struck by Charles Aznavour.
What hit me about him? His fragility, his vulnerability, and that
humble and graceful figure that made me think of St. Francis of
Assisi.

Then I remembered an American novel that I had liked very
much: *Shoot the Piano Player* by David Goodis. But at that time I
was in the middle of shooting *The 400 Blows* and was so worried
that I didn't know if I would ever have the chance to make another film.

A little after the Cannes Festival a friend introduced me to
Charles Aznavour. He seemed very reserved, almost defiant, on the
defensive. I gave him *Shoot the Piano Player* to read and showed
him *The 400 Blows* in a private screening.

I know that Charles is reserved enough to give his confidence
only when it is total and never to be doubted. By temperament he
likes directors who are unlike me, directors who are very precise,
never change their minds, and foresee everything. Yet he never
complained, even when we wrote the dialogue of a scene an hour
before making it, even when we had him in the snow all day without filming. He behaved precisely as if it were his first film. He
didn't have a double for the lights or for the action scenes, and he
worked without makeup.

Translated from "Aznavour donne le 'la,'" Cinémonde, no. 1343
*(May 5, 1960): 36–37. Copyright © 1960 by François Truffaut. Re-
printed by permission of the author.*

Above all I hate the tough guys, the loudmouths, and, in general, all those people, a priori prestigious, who dominate the action as if nothing can touch them. It's not a question of size because big Sterling Hayden is as fragile as little Charles Aznavour: you can read their hearts before you see their muscles. Charles's vulnerability, for example, is like Gabin's used to be, when he didn't necessarily have the "leading man" look, the Gabin of *La Bête Humaine*. Charles in turn has an extraordinary disposition, which lets him give the maximum of truth and simplicity to the most exceptional situations and to accomplish that with a great economy of means. His voice, his gestures, are all there at the beginning.

In *La Tête contre les murs* Charles was a lunar character, poetic but passive. In *Les Drageurs* he was a nonentity. After these two films I thought that he ran the risk of letting himself be locked into these diminished personalities and becoming a prisoner of faggy roles. I mean that one can be weak, fragile, and vulnerable without being a victim; that's why I wanted the main character in *Piano Player* to be very complete: rich, poor, courageous, fearful, timid, impulsive, sentimental, commanding, selfish, tender, soft, and above all, happy in love although never himself taking the first step.

Very well, he's timid, but women adore timid men and throw themselves at them. With each of the three heroines in the film— Marie Dubois, Nicole Berger, and Michèle Mercier—he has a scene in bed. I realized during the making of these scenes that he really was timid because he forced himself to joke, but he was clearly more affected than his partners.

Before filming I was very confident, but I didn't suspect how easy it would be to work with Charles, or the importance of his contribution. It's a little bit with him the way it is with Jean-Pierre Léaud: they both bring such a truth with them that little by little *the film* becomes theirs alone; in both of them you find this strange combination of audacity and humility, aggressiveness and tenderness.

Charles Aznavour isn't easy to "cast" socially; I wouldn't like to see him as a doctor, a detective, or a mechanic; in today's society he's a little on the sidelines, like an emigré or an artist. Therefore I'd like to see him play an emigré artist!

Two parts of him seem a little contradictory: the Charles Aznavour who is calm, measured, reasonable, stable, who doesn't have to reveal himself (that's his Gabin side); and the Charles Aznavour who is foreign, sickly, isolated, a little crazy, moonstruck (that's his Le Vigan* side). Charles has often told me: "The day you need a real nut in a film, call me up."

He is, above all, a poetic person.

If you take a close-up of Charles when he has a neutral look, you will see that when it's shown, this look is full of an infinite unhappiness. That's why I chose for the last shot of *Piano Player* a close-up filmed one day when we had no more time to manage a long scene. And it's because of this sadness that we improvised an unhappy ending.

Charles has great modesty. He tries to give from his depths in a performance, despite the shame of singing or acting, because he is grave and deeply serious; but since he is no less deeply an artist, he couldn't do anything else. He throws himself into the water and gives himself entirely, without trickery.

Finally, I have noticed that all the actors in *Piano Player* were more marvelous in their scenes with Charles than in the scenes in which he did not appear. That explains why everybody likes to work with him: he sounds the right note, he gives the proper tone.

* [Robert Le Vigan, like Jean Gabin, became a film actor in the 1930s. His wide-eyed, often frenzied screen image hinted at a spark of madness within. He and Gabin appeared together in several films, including *Pépe le Moko* (Julien Duvivier, 1936), *The Lower Depths* (Jean Renoir, 1936), and *Quai des Brumes* (Marcel Carné, 1938)—ED.]

The Technique of
SHOOT THE PIANO PLAYER
by KAREL REISZ and GAVIN MILLAR

Truffaut has said in an interview that what he is aiming at is "un éclatement de genres par un mélange de genres"—"an explosion of genres by a mixture of genres." He always tries, he says, to confound his audiences' expectations, to keep them constantly surprised. When the film seems to be going in one direction he likes to turn it round and send it off in another. He thinks of his films as circus shows with a dazzling variety of turns, and likes at the end to take the audience out into the country or to some idyllic scene—snow or the sea—as a reward for being cooped up in the dark for nearly two hours.

It should not be thought that Truffaut is being simply frivolous in saying this. In the first place his films bear out the thesis: each of them[1] does flick from moods of despair to exhilaration and does contain scenes of black comedy alternating with scenes of real tragedy or simply good-hearted unaffected joy. As for locations: the last scene of *Les 400 Coups* has the boy hero running to the sea; the last scene of *Shoot the Pianist* takes place in a snowstorm by a mountain chalet of fairy-tale improbability. *Jules and Jim* is

From The Technique of Film Editing *by Karel Reisz and Gavin Millar, 2nd rev. ed. (London: Focal Press Ltd, 1968), pp. 330–44. Copyright © 1968 by Focal Press, Ltd. Reprinted by permission of the publisher. Title supplied.*

[1] *Les 400 Coups, Tirez sur le Pianiste, Jules et Jim, La Peau Douce, Fahrenheit 451.*

such a lyrical medley of sea, river, alp, and forest that few spectators can surely have suffered from being cooped up with it. *Fahrenheit 451* ends in a snowstorm, in a forest.

Nor are Truffaut's aims the result of simple contrariness. They are the reflection of his philosophy. It is clear from his films that he celebrates what Rhode and Pearson call "the philosophy of discontinuity."

The swift changes of mood and pace which characterize his films are an attempt to match his form more nearly to the way life usually develops. We don't live life according to "genres." Nor is life, according to the way we think today, a taut unbroken chain of significant purposeful acts, linked by logic, as it is sometimes made to appear according to the editing pattern and plot development of the traditional cinema. Indeed, plot often disappears, as it virtually does in *Les 400 Coups*. Antoine's life is described not so much by a series of dramatic events as by a string of nonevents: roaming the streets, playing truant, visiting the fairground, mooning about the flat, avoiding doing his homework.

The action is handled in long unbroken medium shots lasting as long as physically possible. The cuts come when they're unavoidable: when a character leaves the room or goes out of sight down the stairs. It is clear to see from *Les 400 Coups* that Truffaut is a pupil of André Bazin. When the shot lasts too long for comfort, but Truffaut wants to use the beginning and the end, he is not above chopping a bit out of the middle. In one scene involving Antoine's friend and the friend's father, the father goes out of sight through a doorway on his way to the kitchen. He soon reappears in the kitchen, some way away at the end of a dark passage. But between leaving this room and reappearing in the other one there has been a longer time lag than we are led to believe. A cat lazing on a shelf in the top left-hand corner of the frame makes a sudden "jump" to a slightly different position and betrays that there is footage missing. Or it could be that the camera was stopped and locked off in the end position in the first half of the shot and picked up again when the father had had time to get into position for the continuation of the shot. The point is that rather than cut to a new setup, Truffaut tries to preserve the sense of continuity. Similar examples occur elsewhere in *Shoot the Pianist*.

Truffaut disguises a jump cut between two different takes by join-
ing the shots when Fido, the kid-brother, realizes he is being
shadowed by the "crooks" in their big American car. Again, in
Théresa's long, apparently one-shot, confession to Charlie/Edouard
in their flat just before she commits suicide, Truffaut has very
skillfully disguised the fact that he has used the first half of one
take and the second half of another by finding a cutting point where
the images are almost identical for a moment. The question of intention arises. Truffaut confesses that "he saves all his films in the
cutting room." It isn't that these things had never been done before.
But the New Wave directors take more risks, do them more frequently and with more boldness, and more often than not demonstrate that only if the audience is already confused will it be further
confused by unconventional technique.

But in *Les 400 Coups* the mysterious interview with the psychiatric social worker is a classic case of how not to do it, in traditional
terms. During the interview the boy's answers are joined by dissolves and we never see the interviewer at all. As a "dramatic"
scene, or as a treatment of social problems, the scene is a failure.
But of course that isn't its purpose. The real subject is internal and
that is what the method is designed to deal with. The subject is the
boy's own internal world. He takes no interest in the interviewer.
We don't see her because, for him, she hardly exists.

At the end of the film Antoine escapes from the detention center
where he has been sent for stealing a typewriter. He runs to the
sea, which he has never seen. The action is chiefly described in a
very few, very long tracking shots taken from a car while the boy
runs alongside. The sequence lasts several minutes. It is not so
much an event as a state of mind of which the form of the shot is
an apt expression. We feel the freedom of his flight as a great
release after the various sorts of imprisonment, mental and physical,
which he has suffered in the course of the film. In this example,
and in that of the dissolves, too, the form of the shots has been
as much a part of the meaning as any content they have "described."

More so than *Les 400 Coups*, *Shoot the Pianist* extends the
vocabulary of the New Cinema in interesting ways. The story
concerns a concert pianist, Edouard Saroyan, who discovers that
his career really began when his wife slept with his impresario,

Schmeel. She begs his forgiveness, but momentarily he turns from her in disgust. She commits suicide. He retires from society, changes his name to Charlie Koller and becomes a café-player. He has a liaison with a new girl but is once more, after a series of adventures, indirectly the cause of his girl's death.

Charlie goes to Schmeel's flat for an audition. While he is waiting outside the door, he hesitates before pressing Schmeel's bell. He puts out a finger to it, and stops. There then follow two or three bigger and bigger close-ups of his finger and the bell button getting closer. The shots provoke a whole string of reactions: (1) They are funny. (2) They are menacing, as all moments are when the action slows up, or the cutting begins to go into a great deal of detail. So they should be, in view of what we later know is happening (but we don't know it then). (3) They are psychologically accurate since they represent his timidity. (4) They draw attention to a notorious *temps-mort,* that time which we all spend standing outside doors that won't open, or waiting for lifts that won't come. At those moments the universe shrinks to the dimensions of a doorbell which seems for a time to have more reality than oneself. And here we reach perhaps the most central consideration of all. (5) Charlie is a protagonist who embodies the philosophy of discontinuity. His life is a search for wholeness: the wholeness of success, the wholeness of an ideology, of a successful love affair, of a scale of values he can believe in. He looks for confidence and for trust. He doesn't succeed. The representation of his failure is carried in a sequence of images of increasing fragmentation. He is constantly seen reflected in a mirror which hangs over his piano in the café. We are introduced to him in the café's Gents, where he is knotting his tie and looking into the mirror. At the end of the film in the mountain chalet, sheltering from the police after he had accidentally killed a man, he stares into a little cracked shaving mirror and repeats to himself the words of his criminal brother: "Now you are one of us." His relinquishing of himself to Schmeel, the impresario, is marked by the completion of a portrait of him of which Schmeel says, "Thanks to this painting, I can look at you every day." Charlie's wife also speaks of being cut in two by the spider, Schmeel. In the context of this abounding fragmentation, it is not difficult to see the finger-on-bell shots as an indication that for Charlie the universe, the world of objects, is irretrievably breaking up beyond his power to control it.

The opposite process is implied by a similar series of shots in *Jules et Jim,* Truffaut's next film. The shots themselves are three or four simple close-ups of Jeanne Moreau (Catherine) at the driving wheel of her car, switching on, starting up, putting it in gear, and driving off.

Again it is necessary to go into some detail about the story and the theme in order to explain the framework in which to read these shots.

Catherine is beloved by two friends, Jules and Jim. She is a determined experimenter with new forms, not least in love. She is anxious to create new natural forces and combinations, and, for example, to make a *ménage à trois* not only work but appear almost grudgingly ascetic. All three of them do their best to live without jealousy. Jim more actively pursues the affair on his side. Jules, a naturalist, patiently observes, determined, at whatever sacrifice to himself, to hold the circle of friendship unbroken. Catherine, in her vain attempt to create new laws, makes both them and herself unhappy. Finally, she drives her car off the middle of a broken bridge into the river, taking Jim to his death with her. Jules watches from a nearby café terrace.

The film's imagery stresses the naturalness of circular patterns of growth, and the naturalness of plant and insect life. The triangular human relationships fit awkwardly into a cyclical world. In Jules resides the lesson of natural morality: observe and adapt. He hopes, one day, if he is lucky he says, to write a love story in which the characters will be insects. Instead of observing and adapting, Catherine wishes to impose herself on the universe, to adapt it to *her* rather than the other way around. She experiments constantly with the elements. Around her fires are always starting: smoke rises from the vitriol she pours down the sink. When she jumps into the Seine in exasperation one day, little ringlets of reflected light spread out, like fire, across the water. Her attempts to fuse the elements are doomed to failure. Her power to manipulate the material world is only partial. This is where the car-driving close-ups are important. They show her easy mastery of some forms of *artificial* power. But, as if to warn us that this is not enough, the description is fragmented and dislocated out of any possible unity. Gear stick, wheel, accelerator are *tokens* of power only. They bring with them an illusion of mastery. When she drives off the bridge—a broken circle—it is the water, a natural force, which kills her and not the car.[2]

These two examples, from *Shoot the Pianist* and *Jules and Jim,* should show us that even in the, apparently, simple close-up there lies a way into the core of the film's meaning. We are a long way from the days in which the close-up was an answer to the complaint "I can't see what's going on."

Let us look at a sequence from *Shoot the Pianist* which is typical of Truffaut's work in its range of moods and technical dexterity.

Shoot the Pianist[3]

Ft. fr.

1 A newspaper front page which announces the suicide of Thérésa, Charlie's wife. This is superimposed on a barely discernible view of a scrap yard across which the *camera begins to pan right* immediately.

(The newspaper shot has been superimposed on the previous shot of Thérésa lying in the road, dead.) The paper fades and the pan reveals now cars in the junk yard, now a roadway, now a café exterior in a poor quarter.

Newspaper reads: "Wife of 29 noted pianist throws herself from fifth floor."
Charlie's characteristic piano music starts.

Léna's voice
You disappeared. You began a new life. Edouard Saroyan became Charlie Koller. You visited your brothers in the snow and asked them to let Fido live with you. One day you found yourself at Plyne's. *The piano music stops.*

[2] Some of these reflections derive from a fine article about the film: "Elective Affinities" by Roger Greenspun, *Sight and Sound,* Spring 1963.

[3] Director: François Truffaut. Editor: Cécile Decugis. Films de la Pléiade. 1960. Fido, a boy of about twelve, is Charlie's youngest brother. Thérésa is his former wife. Plyne is the proprietor of the café. Léna is a waitress at the café.

Ft. fr.

2 *M.L.S.* Interior café by day. Plyne is mending a table. Charlie is sweeping the floor.

You must have swept that floor 48 6 a thousand times. There was a little upright battered piano in a corner. *A distant engine hoot.* You spent all your time— —looking at it, walking all round it, looking at it again. One day you asked Plyne:

Charlie opens the keyboard.

Charlie:
  Can I play a bit?
Plyne:
  Eh?
Charlie:
  I think I know how.
Plyne:
  Go ahead then. But you better arrange it with Sabine.

Sabine, Plyne's mistress, enters and picks up Charlie's cleaning utensils and walks towards camera. Charlie sits at piano.

3 *B.C.U.* Full face of Charlie, left profile, seated at piano. He looks down at keyboard, serious, then begins to play.
The camera slowly swings right and pans left and tilts down his arms and on to the keyboard. Then it tilts up on to the hammers, seen clearly through the open front of the piano.
MIX TO

43 4

Classical piano music begins.

Music mixes to Charlie's café tune.

4 *M.S.* Interior of café. Nighttime. In a rectangular mirror above the piano Charlie is seen playing. Camera pans down left on to Charlie. He is enjoying himself.

Léna's voice   16
Who is Charlie Koller? Little known. He's a pianist. He looks after his little brother. Above all, he wants no trouble.

5 *M.L.S.* Charlie and two other musicians on the stand. People are dancing.

Thanks to you, the local people 10 8 started coming every evening to dance, and it got to be quite a place. Plyne took on extra staff, and some musicians.

6 *M.C.S.* Victor the drummer.

Victor the drummer, who was 4 8 always laughing without knowing why.

7 *M.C.S.* François the bass player

And his brother François the 3 4 bass player—

8 *C.S.* François's hands on the bass.

—with his long hairy hands. 4 2

9 *M.S.* Exterior of the café. Night.

And then there was me—whom 27

Ft. fr.

The camera begins a *long track-ing shot from left to right* along the pavement outside the café, looking in. It passes over, after a while, the poster on the outside wall advertising "Charlie Koller."

MIX, starting at about 24 ft. and clear in shot 10 at about 30 ft. from the beginning of shot 9.

you looked at all the time with-out ever seeing.

The jaunty music of the café piano gradually mixes to a quieter, more dreamlike theme.

64

10 *M.S.* Interior of bedroom (Léna's). 9 is still panning when 10 begins. 10 too begins with a *pan* which continues throughout the shot, *a full 360 degrees.* But this *pan* is in the opposite direction, i.e., *from right to left.* The shot be-gins on a poster on the wall an-nouncing a concert to be given by Edouard Saroyan. *After 5 ft. of this pan,* a *close-up* of Léna and Charlie kissing each other gently is superimposed and held throughout the shot until, at 54½ ft. in, it starts to disappear. The objects which the pan reveals on its course round the bedroom are in turn, the door, a radio, a window, a bowl of goldfish, a bust (i.e., a piece of sculpture), a bra and other clothes on a chair, and finally the bed with Charlie and Léna in it. The superimposed close-up of them fades completely just before the pan reaches the bed.

11 C.S. Charlie and Léna in bed.

Léna's voice

On my birthday, when I kissed 22 everybody, it was just so that I could kiss you, you know. Then I saw you looking at me, and I looked at you, too.

MIX lasting ½ second.

12 *M.S.* Charlie and Léna in bed, moving in their sleep. *The image is* clear *for little more than a foot.*

MIX lasting ½ second.

2 44

⁴ Since the dissolves are so unusually shot, and the shots too, it isn't very helpful to quote a precise length of shot.

Ft. fr.

13 *As* 11.	What were you thinking about 7 8 when we were walking together in the street last night?
14 *M.S.* As 12, same lengths of dis- solve out of 13 and into 15. *Clear image* for 2 ft. 12 frs. *MIX to*	
15 *C.S. As* 13.	Did you like me right away? 11 Do you remember the evening you said to me—
16 *As* 14 exactly in lengths. *MIX* to	
17 *As* 15.	When I took your arm I was 9 12 afraid you'd be shocked.
18 *As* 16. *Clear for 2 ft. 8 frs.* *MIX* to	
19 *As* 17. *MIX* to	I wanted you so badly to take 7 8 mine.
20 *As* 18. *MIX* to	
21 *C.U.* Léna in bed.	10

The most interesting thing about this extract is that although it
employs a great diversity of styles and tones it has, on the screen,
a surprising homogeneity. This is only partly because of the unity
brought to it by the narrator's voice.[5]

In *1–4* we have moved from Théresa's suicide to Charlie's new
life as the café pianist. In that time we have also established the
locale and tone of the café and learnt a little about its people.
We have learnt especially about Léna's early feeling for Charlie.

[5] The narrator has long been a popular figure in French cinema. He provides
a useful third dimension in addition to the audience and the screen. Or he can
be an objective voice when the "author" wants to comment. The literary parallel
is useful since the narrator is of course a literary device, and the French cinema
has always had a strong literary tradition, which New Wave directors have
generally been keen to preserve. The narrator is also a popular figure in the
American thriller-school, a tradition that the New Wave have equally revered.
Perhaps an interim stage of adoption can be seen in such films as Melville's
Bob Le Flambeur (1956), which is intermittently narrated. At any rate the
narrator makes frequent appearances in the contemporary French cinema, no-
tably in Truffaut's third film, *Jules et Jim.*

All the four shots seem leisurely. *1* and *3* especially have a strong lyrical feeling in them. But they still perform a valuable function in conveying information and drawing character.

Shot *1* associates the sadness and squalor of Théresa's death (she had thrown herself from a window) with the junkyard of old cars, by having the newspaper superimposed over both shots. The junkyard suggests the spiritual depths to which Charlie has been plunged by his wife's suicide. It also tells us, of course, what sort of area he has chosen to bury himself in in order to get away from the bright lights and all his former friends. Léna's affectionate regard comes through in the commentary (especially in the description of Charlie's fascination by the piano), but the lightness of tone is not allowed to detract from the seriousness with which we are to treat Charlie. In the next shot his excellence as a pianist is brought to our attention by the intensity of the moving close-up, which seems to give him dignity. In no way does this cast any reflection on Léna's slight playfulness about him. It is this constant delicacy in balancing tones of feeling, in commentary/dialogue and image, which gives Truffaut's film the curious flavor of sadness and joy which it has.

In the next section the jokes are about, but not at the expense of, Victor and François. Charlie, in *4* and *5*, is happily jogging in time to the music. But they are not just jokes. Léna is talking about the three of them, and so we see Charlie at the piano, then the three on the stand, then Victor, then François, and François's hairy hands. But when she mentions herself it seems to be her characteristic modesty which prevents her from appearing when we should most expect it. Instead of her we see the exterior of the café, and in a long tracking shot past the windows, watch the happy couples inside. It is almost as though Léna is silently telling us that she feels she is shut out from this happiness. We know that that is how Charlie feels about his own life. A link between them is tacitly suggested, almost entirely by the absence of an expected shot, and the form of another.

But the exterior tracking shot is not simply a metaphorical device. The shot continues until we pan across a poster announcing the attraction of "Charlie Koller" playing at the café. With perfect logic this suggests the poster of Edouard Saroyan which we know is hanging in Léna's bedroom. In a curious dissolve the poster of Saroyan, with something of a metaphorical force, since it represents as it were the wishes of Léna, appears to displace the stand-in, Charlie Koller. So we see, too, that the movement of the camera along the pavement and away from the café was a way of expressing the movement of Léna's mind away from the café and towards her own bedroom where she lies now with Charlie.

The dissolve is curious because, breaking all the rules, it not only begins at the end of *9* on movement, not only continues in *10* on movement, but the movements are in opposite directions. The effect mixes the images in such a way as to suggest pleasant reverie, though it doesn't pretend that it is a picture of what Léna herself is seeing.

The pan from the poster of Saroyan on the bedroom wall is the longest shot in the sequence. Because of the close-up of Charlie and Léna superimposed over it, the underlying images of the bedroom are hard to discern. This is what makes the moment when the goldfish bowl swims into view particularly delicate. For a few seconds as the camera pans over them, the four goldfish are seen, in long shot, nibbling the surface of the water in exactly the same way as the lovers are nuzzling each other's faces. The superimposition disappears just before the pan completes its circle and we come back to the bed again. The next eleven shots are a most unusual device. The short alternate shots into and out of which we dissolve so quickly show the lovers stirring vaguely in the abandoned attitudes of sleep. They take liberties with our conventional idea of the time scale, and they work, literally, like a charm.

Through the Looking Glass
by ROGER GREENSPUN

Uneven, mangled, wobbly melodrama about barroom pianist
who gets involved with hoodlums. Satire and spoofs never quite
come off. [Capsule review of *Shoot the Piano Player* almost any
week in *Cue*.]

If there is any unifying tone in the film it is an existential
irrelevance, coupled with a shrug from Charles Aznavour, a
masterful actor, which asks, What did you expect? Existence is a
succession of dirty jokes: nothing lasts, struggle is futile, hope
is obscene. (The title *Shoot the Piano Player* refers to a barroom
sign in old Westerns—"Don't Shoot the Piano Player"—but Truffaut's film might as easily be called *Why Not Shoot the Piano
Player?*) [Judith Shatnoff in *Film Quarterly*, Spring 1963.]

And Truffaut himself is so completely engaged in life that he
pleads for the piano player's right to be left alone, to live in his
withdrawn state, *to be out of it.* Truffaut's plea is, of course,
"Don't shoot the piano player." [Pauline Kael in *Film Culture
no. 27*.]

But Turley banged his hands against his knees. "Why ain't
you there?"

"Because I'm here," Eddie said. "I can't be two places at
once." [David Goodis, *Down There*.]

A return to *Shoot the Piano Player* now, long after the impact
of its initial showing and, I hope, long before its enshrinement as

From Moviegoer, *1 (Winter 1964). Copyright © 1964 by Roger Greenspun. Reprinted by permission of the author.*

a classic, requires some explanation. *Piano Player* has enjoyed exceptional popular success, bucking Bosley Crowther in the art circuits and at least in New York filtering down to some neighborhood houses; it has excited everybody worth exciting; but among critics it seems to have inspired more enthusiasm for its moods than understanding of its meaning. That it makes some kind of meaning, despite Truffaut's own not very helpful post mortem comment that although a lot goes on in his film there is no theme you can put your finger on,[1] and that such meaning has to do with matters other than whether or not to shoot the piano player, a question obviously designed to be let go begging, is the underlying point to these remarks.

What I have to say will owe something to the most suggestive single commentary on Truffaut I know, Michel Delahaye's fine review of *Jules and Jim* in *Cahiers du Cinéma*, No. 129. *Piano Player* embraces a phenomenology of extraordinary proportions: when a man's inner withdrawal creates a void in nature into which his wife then actually falls, theme and event become effectively indistinguishable, and my notions of how to account for the connections between them derive partly from Delahaye's insights into Truffaut's exploitation of visual-verbal puns and inversions.

I

So much happens in the Truffaut films that it is difficult even for a moment to draw back from their engrossing busyness and fix upon a single image in any one of them for a long close look. But it is a useful thing to do if you wish to isolate a revealing characteristic, and conveniently each of the three features gives us such an image at its very end. One remembers Antoine alone at the water's edge, caught in a still photograph with nowhere further to run, at the end of *The 400 Blows;* or Jules, his back to the camera, striding alone down the path of the cemetery where he has just

---

[1] In an interview analyzing audience reaction in *Cahiers du Cinéma* No. 138. Excerpts are translated in *Film Quarterly*, Fall 1963.

interred his wife and his best friend; or the noncommittal face of Charlie Koller, almost filling half the screen, appearing at the end of *Shoot the Piano Player* over the same honky-tonk tune with which the film had opened.

The first of these scenes reduces its film to stasis, the second prefigures escape, and the third suggests that everything moves around in a circle to come back pretty much to where it began. The music of Albert's ballad behind the retreating figure of Jules; Charlie's picking up the piano tune once again—by signalling an end to eventful progression both function in a way analogous to Antoine's stopping the movie. And each of the scenes contains a single character, not the suggestive grouping of even two characters in significant relation, so that we are left not with the figurative resolution of a drama but rather with just one figure, a man central to his world (as I think Jules rather than Catherine is for *Jules and Jim*) but bereft of that world's potential for sustaining and varying events. That each of these characters in certain particulars reproduces Antoine, desperately childlike in his need for the motherly attention of the woman who has for some reason been denied him, is thematically interesting for Truffaut's work so far. But perhaps *as* interesting is the final emphasis upon the man himself rather than upon any conclusive configuration to an action. I think it is fair to say that the Truffaut films develop activity rather than an Aristotelian "action," that they are concerned with making things happen rather than with the disposing of events in a dramatic structure, that by their own inner necessity they must at last center upon the actor—he who acts, or causes things to happen—and that they do not so much end as run down, or run on in what is pretty clearly to be mere repetition.

Like *Jules and Jim, Piano Player* includes the telling of many stories: the normal happy life account of the man with the flowers, Chico's hard luck story in the café, the central flashback story of Edouard and Théresa, Théresa's own story of her shame, the crooks' crazy stories to Charlie and Léna and later to Fido, the story of the whole clan of the ill-fated Saroyans—going back generations, Charlie supposes, before one can discover the root of their curse. And, as in *Jules and Jim*, such an abundance of narratives seems partly to free the film as a whole from dependency upon any one story as basic structure, and to work for the suspension of "narrative," among other elements, within some different kind of form.

The problem is to describe the form, and here Michel Delahaye offers a clue in a few brilliant demonstrations. He notices, for example, that when Fido drops his milk bomb upon the hood of Ernest and Momo's car, they are obliged to turn on the windshield wipers to combat *"l'opacité de cette blancheur qui risque de faire obstacle à leurs noirs desseins"* [the opacity of this whiteness which stands in the way of their black designs]. Thus Delahaye assumes not only that whiteness darkens, but also that between the *visible* whiteness of the milk-spattered windshield and the conventional *ideas* of "black designs" there is a viable punning relation. The virtuosity of Delahaye's formulation is immediately matched and deepened by the movie, for not only are Ernest and Momo literally rendered dark by the white milk screen cutting off enough available light to make them no more than silhouettes, but their own evil "blackness" is within minutes made bright by their lively talking with Charlie and Lena in the initial kidnapping. Thus white opposes black, but white also makes black; and white and black are relative not only to one another but also within themselves—each showing a range of highlights and shadows once it is opened to close inspection. The enabling principle here is not the moral collapsing of black in white—which shades too readily in the minds of some critics to a gray acceptance of all conduct— but rather the fruitful notion of division into opposites itself, a multiplying of distinctions between and within spheres, of which black and white is only one manifestation, although a significant one for a film *in* black and white with the piano keyboard as one of its operative images.

Elsewhere I have attempted identifying abstract figures in *Jules and Jim*[2] and I have suggested that for that film, moving broadly through historic time, the circle ultimately is the lively restful figure containing and supporting the abundance of life that everyone has seen somehow as its central value. But *Piano Player* is antihistorical, destroying time in the mirror image of its long

[2] In *Sight and Sound,* Spring 1963.

flashback, moving in all directions through space, and finding its impetus to movement in the idea of cutting things up—dividing them so as to set part against part in a series of gestures that literally split the screen. *Piano Player* is also full of circles: but notice that each of them, whether in the actual insets of the triple-faced Plyne, Ernest's mother dropping dead, or suave Lars Schmeel ominously fading out between Edouard and Theresa in bed—or in the lyrical slow pan of Lena's room which shares the screen with a stationary shot showing Charlie and Lena kissing beneath an inverted horse-shoe[3]—promotes a consciousness of discreet visual elements.

II

The catastrophes that invariably attend Charlie's major with-drawals—according to the principle of multiple relations I have borrowed from Delahaye, by which ideas, things, and images enjoy equality as phenomena—demonstrate the law that nature abhors a vacuum, at the same time that they enforce a plunge into the midst of events once again, restarting the round of activity in which the film lives. Quite simply: Edouard runs out on Theresa after her eloquent admission of emptiness, and her body tumbles into the void he might have filled; Charlie splits from Lena at a cru-cial juncture, and her rush to mend the break ends with her sliding dead down a snowy hillside; even Plyne sinks into the circle of his own crushing embrace after Charlie tries calling it quits.

On the level of human motivation Charlie's fatal attractiveness to women relates to the need everybody in the film seems to feel for somebody else. The easy and real contact made and broken between Chico and the man who helps him at the beginning, Ernest and Momo's need not just to kidnap people but to make friends with them, the brute expression of Plyne's lonely frustration, even the ironic pathos with which Edouard looks for the real pianist in a bedroom mirror—all catch some aspect of a drive towards com-

---

[3] For the record, there is another bad luck sign, a cracked mirror in the Saroyans' country kitchen. Charlie comes upon it just as his brothers joyfully confirm his membership in the clan.

pletion not in self-sufficiency but in personal contact. The amount of self-expression granted Clarisse, Plyne, the brothers, and so many others has more to it than an undeniable delight in character for its own sake; it is also a bid for bridging a gap that always threatens to appear beneath a surface that must be kept full and close if it is not to fail. When Charlie asks Lena for what reason she wants to back him in a return to the concert stage, she answers, not *"pourquoi"* but *"pour qui. Pour moi et pour vous, pour nous deux."*

Charlie's fatal attractiveness has its dark and unique underside as fate—in every woman who advances his career, from the old lady who used to drive him to his piano lessons and away from his brothers, to the mysterious girl with the violin who opens the door to Lars Schmeel's office for him when he is just about to back away —but it is not otherwise so very different from the mutual attractiveness of one for another that permeates the movie, and that finds its typical expression in everyone's telling somebody else part of a life story. Only Charlie clams up, and then people obligingly either tell him his own story (Lena), or make up stories for him (Lars Schmeel), or give him advice on how to improve his story (Schmeel and Plyne). But his own rich life is inward; his deepest dialogues are with himself. In response to Theresa's moving and articulate confession he can only rush out of the room. While he lies in Lena's arms—by the cutting that alternates two time sequences in the course of their love-making—he is in fact already turning away from her while she recounts the history of her attempts to move toward him.

The headlong falls on the way to Charlie that occur in *Piano Player* climax this preoccupation, and equalize planes of expression that in most films have at best no more than a metaphoric relation. Here every gesture takes place in space, or, better, makes the space in which and by which subsequent acts exist. There is no saying that character and situation influence one another; they *are* one another. It is therefore with the authority of image raised to the power of theme, and theme raised to the power of image, that the principle of division vitalizes and ultimately threatens this world. Split into a series of more or less precise oppositions, the strange career of Charlie/Edouard shuttles on, potentially into an infinity of mutually reflecting mirror images.

III

Theresa falls from a very great height. She leaps from the pinnacle to which she has been instrumental in raising her husband (the later parts of their story are largely seen in sequences of walking up and down stairs) both into the void she finds within herself and into the gap he has made in their perfect union, where they were so many things to each other—husband and wife, student and teacher, waitress and customer—in a life game in which, as Schmeel neatly observes, everybody is a winner. Edouard turned Charlie completes her fall, descending down beneath the dark roadway where she dies to the absolute blackness of the cellar he is hidden in after killing Plyne. Together with Lena he ascends again, up into the bright sunlight and snow of the mountains, only to witness another fall beginning his own second descent.

The stories' similarity in spatial outline is completed by various complementary or opposing details: the two impresarios, Plyne and Schmeel, both sure they know what's wrong with Charlie and both after his women; Edouard's desertion of Theresa because she is sullied, and Charlie's defense of Lena after Plyne brands *her* as sullied; Theresa's loss of identity after Schmeel's attack, and Plyne's insistence that a Lena who speaks foul language is not a woman; a blond waitress in one story and a dark one in the other, but a dark death for the blond and a snowy white one for the brunette; a romantic tale of dedicated love and brilliant success supported by a grimy business deal, and an obscure and sordid life briefly illumined by a recklessly romantic dream.

Two stories, two parts of a life divided up to escape itself, so ingeniously reproducing one another, do more than give the film the air of fatality that persistently dogs Charlie and that finds general expressive outlet in virtually everything from the tough-luck café ballad on up. A major part of their function is realized in the very creation of a pair of reflecting surfaces, which, by their extensive relations to one another, enclose the *Piano Player* world within an apparently hermetic seal of correspondences. Within this enclosure it is hopeless to look for resolution. Charlie necessarily seeks his way through and out, and his famous withdrawal tendencies owe as much to the kind of space he occupies as to any quirk in his own character. Getting a real grip on Charlie is no easy task, as Plyne, Schmeel, Ernest and Momo, and any number of film critics all demonstrate—and as the piano player discovers for himself.

Who *is* Charlie Koller? He is Edouard Saroyan. Who is Edouard Saroyan? A brilliant concert pianist. Is he? Edouard himself asks the question—of the critics, of Hemingway (does he collect my records?), of the janitor, of himself as he stands before a mirror hoping to catch an image of the real thing but seeing only the face that asks the question thrown back at him. Schmeel says that at last he "has" Edouard when he has a portrait painted, the dark figure of a pathetic man against a dark background. But just as Schmeel makes his boast the portrait is totally obscured, not by a deeper darkness but by brilliant flashes of light from news photographers —so that it too becomes a reflecting surface, revealing nothing at all. The problem of identity, the reliable place of a man among the things and events of his world, remains unsolved, but it remains the major problem in the film.

During the sequence with Schmeel and the portrait, Edouard does something typical: he moves from in front of the photographers' flash bulbs (*they* don't catch him; they catch a pose imitated from the man in the poster who has ideally conquered timidity) to the darkest recess of Schmeel's office, which is itself an arrangement in sharp intervals of bright windows and dark interstices —like the piano keyboard, like the double life, an alternation of black and white. *All* Charlie/Edouard's movements are between these extremes. To attempt making some controlled associations for black and white is to begin seeing the inclusive mode of *Piano Player,* and, in determining the potential for characterization of that mode, to work towards the conditions for life it fosters.

IV

Edouard and Charlie, Theresa and Lena, Schmeel and Plyne, wealth and poverty, success and failure, light and darkness—these mirror another, touch, interpenetrate, but never enter into solution. Simply to look at *Piano Player* is to exercise a heightened awareness of contrast, beginning with a single spotlight cutting through a field of black, reaching a climax in the breathtakingly beautiful ride from Paris to the mountains—highway lights in the darkness, reflections off the windshield of Lena's car, brilliant sunlight on a high snowy landscape—and ending in the screen's strict vertical division into black and white.

To the extent that the *idea* of black and white hovers over the film, available for any new improvisation, it engenders and supports all activity, but actually explains none of it. It is pattern, and not morality or psychology or antipsychology, though it may lend itself to any of these for the time it takes to complete a gesture or establish an attitude. But this impartial vituosity exacts a toll upon the characters whose lives it activates but whose human responses it does not quite account for. There is a tension in the film that exceeds the potential of the brilliant determinism I have been describing, and that derives from a feeling but utterly unsentimental understanding of the complexities of lives that are caught in the proliferation of mutually exclusive terms their world offers. Everybody in *Piano Player* is an articulate spokesman for a way of life, but almost everybody understands life as a selection from among absolute commitments. Charlie accepts Clarisse for bed and board but completely rejects her for anything else, Plyne knows exactly what is and what is not a woman, Schmeel divides and conquers— and so on through a range of demonstration that finds in the making of distinctions one of the film's crucial preoccupations. The corollary of so much picking of sides is a special kind of picking apart; the end of sharp distinctions is finally disintegration. And this is the burden of a speech given a moment before death, Theresa's set confession, structurally at the center of the film, movingly describing a failure in personal integration that many people at one time or another feel but that only she totally articulates.

With perfect instinct, Truffaut has utilized most of the events in David Goodis's miserable novel, merely moving them from New York and Philadelphia to Paris, while rejecting almost all its interpretations of them. The one great exception is Theresa's confession, where he has retained and elaborated upon a body of dialogue that remains isolated as pathos in the novel [4] but meaningfully connects with everything in the film. Theresa describes Schmeel's precisely calculated method of attack, and the change, the loss of the old Theresa, it has made in her. Schmeel has taken her body and discarded her heart; the seduction has been an operation. He has left no visible scar; Schmeel slides out as efficiently as he slides in, and there have been no complications. But in the midst of a gleaming world—white sports car, white apartment, bright lights, shining blond girl—she discovers darkness and filth. A few scenes before, Edouard had looked in the mirror to find himself, and now she reveals that she has looked too—but there is no Theresa anywhere, only a used up dirty old rag. Schmeel has come and gone, but for her what she did yesterday is part of what she is today. "Yesterday" is her mirror, and it is different in quality from anybody else's. She looks specifically for an emotional continuity to life, and her way of describing the destruction of that continuity—the dissolution of bright surfaces and an awareness of encroaching night—provides something very like a point of moral reference for the film's methods. Every death in *Piano Player* follows an analogous pattern, but only Theresa's is self-willed, a conscious recognition of the despair that accompanies the pattern, finding between its sharp distinctions the crack that opens to the abyss of total nonbeing, personal annihilation.

In this complex of surfaces any face is a mask, and every mask presupposes a secret life behind it. Charlie's two secret lives, the one he's leading and the one he's keeping secret, are of course the film's central stories; but other lives and stories have their place. (There are even fleeting suggestions of potential integration—in the late-discovered love and growing family of the stranger who helps Chico up after his collision with a lamppost, the first tumble in the movie and visually, with its dark night and flowers as against morning light and snow, an inverted counterpart of the last; or in the enthusiastic acceptance with which the other Saroyan brothers, great antidivisionists on principle, welcome back Edouard even with the cops probably on his tail, now that he has killed a man and is one of them.) But when the stories are over and the secret

[4] Pp. 80–82 in the Grove Press Black Cat edition.

lives have mostly been exposed into obscurity, some faces still remain. As Chico tells Plyne very early, you don't get any information without paying for it; and if one of Charlie's women describes the apprehension of death for her world, the other dies to give it its image—in a terrifying slow dissolve that superimposes the dead face of Lena upon the movie's closing sequence. What we feel at this moment is not so much the pathos of Lena's pointless killing as the authority of death itself. The face that looks back at us from the snow, an inverted image to be sure, conceals no secret at all. What you can see is all there is to it, and that is quite enough. Lena's perfect containment, like Theresa's total emptiness, is a cipher—but one or the other is all there is to discover when the running, fighting, loving, playing, remembering stop.

People have been so busy admiring Truffaut's marvelous inventiveness and vitality that they have ignored the fact that each of his films, beginning with the initiation to manhood through contact with death in *Les Mistons* (*The Mischief-makers*), is finally about the failure, the turning stale, of inventiveness and vitality. The three features seal this point by turning their child-man protagonists into emblems of life possibilities exhausted; and especially in *Piano Player* the emblem is fully, schematically developed. A wide screen divided down the middle into white and black, the line of the piano top across the bottom, Charlie's impassive face against the dark—the resources of film itself, the terms of this film's life, the man positioned to one side, and the machine for banging out the tune spanning both sides, holding the world together, keeping things going for the time being.

COMMENTARIES

Adapting
SHOOT THE PIANO PLAYER
by FRANÇOIS TRUFFAUT

I don't like my films, except the sketch in *Love at Twenty*. I
know their problems, their development, the intentions, and the
result. Sometimes I'm unhappy with the intentions or the result,
but I'm always convinced that I would like them much more if
they had been made by someone else, because then I would see
only the intentions and the annoyances that occurred in the course
of filming. Abel Gance says that when you make a film, you get
onto the screen 10 percent of what you wanted to do, although I
wouldn't make it the same proportion. Perhaps my dreams are less
frenzied than Gance, but I do believe that I achieve on the screen
only part of what I wanted to do, and in the case of *Piano Player*,
it's very hazy. Yet, as a spectator seeing the film, I'd love it because
I like what's gone into it. I prefer American films that are dubbed
and that's the feeling I get from this film. Everything that people
do and say, all their intentions, the little cabin—I just adore it.
In fact, I know it's not normal for them to go out in the snow in
the middle of the day and then suddenly talk about going and
hiding (we had so many problems with this film), but in fact, speaking as a critic, I like that better than "successful" films that don't
agree with my state of mind.

I couldn't adapt a film from a book I hated. Even if I don't like

Excerpted and translated from "Ce qu'a dit François Truffaut,"
Cinéma 67, no. 112 (January 1967): 41–44. *Reprinted by permission of*
Cinema 67. *Title supplied.*

the style of a book, I can tell myself: "The style doesn't matter; it's the facts that count." But you can't do that. Because the irritation that style brings out in me sprouts so well that each time a producer gave me a book to read, even if there was a synopsis, I had to say no, because the resumé that somebody made didn't seem to me to have any flesh and I think that a book could be adapted only for its stylistic qualities. It's a little dangerous to talk about how an image is equivalent, but still . . . I like a lot of things in Goodis: characters, action, and the style he writes in. For example. Théresa's confession before she commits suicide is something I would be incapable of writing or even imagining. If some scriptwriter friend brought it to me, I'd refuse it . . . and still she's what she is. She is exactly as she is in the book. But sometimes there is more than one influence . . . I remember that I wanted to do the book because I admired it. At the time of *The 400 Blows* and all the euphoria at Cannes, I told Braunberger that there was a book I really wanted to do, which I really enjoyed when I read it several years before; I also liked Aznavour very much and thought, well, if we can put two good things together, let's do it! Braunberger bought the rights and made a contract with Aznavour. Subsequently, as I was rereading the book, I realized that I had made a reckless decision. The book really required a very strong character, a character with physical presence like Sterling Hayden. And the famous scene when he kills Plyne in the bar is a scene that had been based on the principle of the strong man toying with his prey without taking advantage of it; but the other man (Plyne) has a knife and the main character has to kill him in spite of himself.

This whole idea dissolved because of the choice of Aznavour. I was tormented for several days. Then I changed direction. That's why I contacted Marie Dubois for the role of Léna. I said to myself: "You have to go to the exact opposite and take a girl who will be stronger than he and who will carry him on her shoulders, this guy who's as light as a feather. That opposition would clear everything up." And we were able to work it out. Sometimes there were still other influences. When I saw the film again, I remembered that there's a whole part of Aznavour's relationship with Nicole Berger that's influenced by Moravia's *Contempt*. It's the story of a woman who has facilitated her husband's success; he thinks she's contemptuous of him. This appears in the first scenes with Nicole Berger. That's why you can say that this genre of film is an amalgam, filled with references to the American films I've loved. The strongest influence was Nicholas Ray's *Johnny Guitar.*

The adaptation was made very casually. The end in the snow was worked out among ourselves. Albert Rémy, Daniel Boulanger, and I were sitting around a table and wondering who's going to shoot whom. Down there the cold weather had taken its toll of the cast, and we decided to shoot with those who weren't sick. Finally we quickly killed off the ones who had to go back to Paris. The whole end was made that way, with the one exception that, despite the friendly insistence of Braunberger, I had planned to have Marie Dubois die; so beforehand I had filmed the small section of the final scene where there's a new waitress.

Another influence was Audiberti. I was rather sad that he hadn't liked *The 400 Blows,* and that he hadn't dared tell me. In general, he liked everything and never rejected anything. One day he told me: there's a Simenon aspect there that bothers me. It also lacks something else, the idea that it's only a story." I thought about Audiberti during the filming of *Piano Player,* and a part of Plyne's character is clearly influenced by him. I said to myself: "This one has to be a character like Audiberti, who has a completely magical idea of young people." At that moment there's a reversal in the film. You realize that the sympathetic and timid little guy isn't so shy after all and copes pretty well, and that the true victim of Society is someone who puts women on a pedestal, like Audiberti and the barowner had. There the film is more influenced by Audiberti's own character than by his books.

It's not necessary to look for reality in *Piano Player*—neither in the Armenian family in the snow near Grenoble, nor in the bar in Levallois-Perret—(there's really no dancing in that kind of bar). All I wanted was the pleasure of mixing things together to see whether or not they were miscible. I strongly believe in this idea of mixing. I think it controls everything.

I don't want to compare the two films at all—mine is a *divertissement*—but I think that in *Hiroshima* Resnais's pleasure was to see if you could mix the story of the atomic bomb with the story of a girl in Nevers who had her hair sheared at the Liberation because she slept with a German. Resnais wanted to see if the two things were miscible, his work then being to make them mix. But it couldn't be accepted in that film. The idea of acceptance is also important. Otherwise you could do anything, leave the screen white, or leave it black. Your interest, when you make that kind of bet, is to win.

François Truffaut and
SHOOT THE PIANO PLAYER
by ROY ARMES

Tirez sur le Pianiste (1960) was a far freer work [than *The 400 Blows*], derived from an American *série noire* thriller by David Goodis. In their adaptation of this work Truffaut and Marcel Moussy were faced with a most implausible plot concerning the double life of a pub pianist Charlie Kohler (played by Charles Aznavour), who had once been a successful concert pianist, Edouard Saroyan. The Edouard half, told in flashback as Charlie reveals it to his second love Léna, is pure melodrama, treating the hero's reliationship with his wife who sacrificed her honor to give him his chance and then committed suicide. By contrast, the scenes of the hero's subsequent life as Charlie are handled in a loose, humorous, and affectionate manner, full of irrelevancies and parody. They show Charlie's involvement, through his brother Chico, with a couple of wildly improbable pipe-smoking gunmen (Daniel Boulanger and Claude Mansard). On the run after accidentally killing the pubowner in a brawl over Léna, Charlie joins up with his brothers in the lonely family farmhouse, but when the gunmen arrive in pursuit of Chico, it is Léna who gets shot and dies amid the snow.

As is inevitable in a work of this nature it is the comic elements

From French Cinema Since 1946, vol. 2: The Personal Style *by Roy Armes (New York: A. S. Barnes & Co., 1966) pp. 58–59, 65–69. Reprinted by permission of A. S. Barnes & Co., and The Tantivy Press. Title supplied.*

127

that come across best in *Tirez sur le Pianiste*—the characterization
of the gangsters, the opening sequence of Chico's conversation with
a total stranger, the crazy song of Bob Lapointe concluding "Vanille
et framboise sont les mamelles du destin." The characterization of
the two women who figure in Charlie's life and for whose deaths he
is largely responsible is sound if unexciting, and the playing of
Nicole Berger as the wife and Marie Dubois as Léna is excellent.
The chief flaw lies in the central character, for the two halves of
Charlie-Edouard's life never coalesce, despite the sympathetic playing of Charles Aznavour. He is consecutively typical Truffaut hero
(hesitantly accosting Léna), *série noire* hero (sleeping with a statu-
esque prostitute who worships him, and killing the pubowner
Plyne), and melodramatic concert pianist (thumping out Chopin in
the Salle Pleyel, and watching his wife leap to her death). Not sur-
prisingly we never feel that the various aspects add up to a single
coherent character.

In a similar way the film as a whole is disjointed, constantly
changing its moods and continually surprising the audience with a
new turn of the plot or a fresh idea. This makes the film lively
and entertaining but lessens the impact of the more serious passages. The final transition to solemnity, when Léna is killed after a
parody of a gunfight, is flatly handled and leaves the spectator un-
moved. For a time Truffaut's verve and the technical flourish of
his director of photography, Raoul Coutard, can conceal the absurdities of plot and characterization, but in the end the lack of
conviction about the whole work is only too apparent . . .

The work of François Truffaut oscillates between the extremes of
personal involvement and artificial *série noire* contrivance. At times
he makes films which fit clearly into one category or the other—*Les
Quatre Cents Coups* or *La Mariée était en Noir*—but very often
there is an overlap, as in *Jules et Jim,* where the work of adaptation
leaves plenty of scope for the expression of his own personality or
in *La Peau Douce* where an original story is given an ending of
B-picture melodramatics. Throughout his work the two types of
film-making alternate, with the highly personal *Baisers Volés* sand-
wiched between two adaptations of thrillers by William Irish. Yet
this is not really a result of commercial pressures, for Truffaut has
been able to maintain his independence over ten years of film-

making. Though he lacks the freedom and fluency of Godard, he has still managed to avoid the decline to mere routine forced upon Chabrol by the failure of his films at the box office, and his own company, Les Films du Carrosse, has been involved in all his film-making ventures. If Truffaut chooses thriller material it is clearly because of his own predilections and a certain lack of confidence in totally personal expression. He once told an interviewer: "The worse thing when you are the complete author of a film is that you are more troubled by doubts"—a statement of a kind inconceivable from Godard or Antonioni or Bresson.

Truffaut's admiration for the work of Alfred Hitchcock is perhaps a clue to his continuing concern with construction and audience involvement. Talking specifically of *Tirez sur le Pianiste* and *Jules et Jim* Truffaut once defined his approach in circus terms:

> My films *are* circus shows, and that's what I want them to be. I'd never show two elephant acts running. After the elephant comes the conjuror; after the conjuror, the bear. I even arrange an interval round about the sixth reel because people may be getting a bit tired. At the seventh reel I take them in hand again, and try to end up with the best thing in the show . . . I swear I'm not joking: I really do think about the circus while I'm working. I'd like people to boo the sequences that have gone wrong and clap the ones they enjoy.

This definition explains perfectly the unevenness of the two films involved. They are episodic by intention and a commentary is used not to give a rhythm (in the manner of Resnais) or to probe a central character (as in Bresson's films) but simply to link together the various fragments. For the changes of mood to work so smoothly depth must be avoided, and the transitions are not from farce to tragedy but from the amusing to the sad. The strange lack of unity in *Tirez sur le Pianiste* can be explained by the fact that the two halves of Charlie Kohler's life are deliberately kept as distinct as possible, for otherwise there would be "two elephant acts running." The same approach is still visible in the handling of the five murders in *La Mariée était en Noir* which are differentiated to provide variety rather than to offer depth of psychological analysis.

Truffaut's fatal unwillingness to commit himself to use the camera to probe is at the root of the most characteristic feature of his style up to *La Peau Douce*—the sweeping camera movement. In films like *Tirez sur le Pianiste* and *Jules et Jim* the truth of the details and moments caught so well by Raoul Coutard's camera gives the surface appearance of life, but the very mobility of the camerawork prevents the characters from being pinned down and examined in depth. Truffaut's world is one where happiness is expressed in motion: if his characters have no cares, they run across the fields, roll downhill, zoom by on their bicycles, and the camera moves in order to keep up with them. In *Jules et Jim* the joy of Catherine and Jim in their new-found love is similarly expressed by great sweeping camera movements over the woods around Jules's house, shot from a helicopter. But life is not all happiness and when some more serious moment occurs Truffaut's method fails. In the same film one of the key scenes is that in which Catherine learns that Jim is going to marry someone else and that his feelings for her are dead. She is brought by this to face up to the truth about her whole way of life: "Et moi, Jim?" This should be a moment of revelation, but instead Truffaut changes the mood. There is a burst of ominous music, Catherine seizes a revolver, Jim leaps from the window and rushes away. The moment is lost and the possibility of giving Catherine a new dimension has vanished. For this reason his best work does take the form of comedy in which this kind of involvement would be irrelevant.

It is arguable that the things Truffaut is least good at are those he derives from the thrillers he admires so much. If his films contain so many deaths (three in *Tirez sur le Pianiste,* two in *Jules et Jim,* one in *La Peau Douce,* six in *La Mariée était en Noir*) this is less an expression of his personality than a bad habit picked up during years of seeing and admiring B-pictures. Truffaut's film endings (apart from *Les Quatre Cents Coups*) are weak because death is not a thing that can be encompassed in his scheme of things and therefore appears as an ill-fitting appendage: "I have realised that I cannot invent anything violent because I do not dare to. I dare not introduce a revolver, a gun; I dare not imagine a suicide, a death; so I remain in the everyday world, if I write scenarios alone or with a friend. Yet, I like to see exceptional things in films and I like filming them if I have found them already written." Truffaut is clearly attracted by the idea of portraying exceptional beings like Charlie Kohler in *Tirez sur le Pianiste* or Julie Kohler in *La Mariée était en Noir*, but there is little attempt at probing a tormented mind. Instead Truffaut uses the situation to provide ideal roles for star performers like Aznavour or Jeanne Moreau. His ability to handle performers in this way is perhaps best illustrated in *Baisers Volés* by the glamour radiated by Delphine Seyrig.

The criminal aspects of Truffaut's material are best when incorporated into the more personal style of the Antoine Doinel films: *Les Quatre Cents Coups, L'Amour à Vingt Ans,* and *Baisers Volés,* where juvenile delinquency is blended with a farcical school atmosphere or the whole idea of detection and investigation happily parodied. Except in the adaptations like *Fahrenheit 451* and *La Mariée était en Noir,* when he is totally absorbed in plot development, he concentrates on the surface of life. He is not at all at home with general ideas; for example, he offers no social or political comment: "In effect, I don't tackle the 'problems of our time' in my films, and if I did try to tackle them I would be incapable of 'taking up an attitude.' It's a matter of temperament. The characters in a film interest me more than the story, so I can't make a film of ideas." His own personal interests hardly rise beyond the trivial, the ordinary, the everyday: "It's in the territory of journalism that these 'urgent' things belong and are best expressed . . . Personally I have chosen fiction. This doesn't exclude ideas about life, about the world, about our society. But I like everything which muddles the trail, everything which sows doubts . . . I enjoy unexpected details, things that prove nothing, things that show how vulnerable men are." This is, of course, the aspect of life which his films capture best. The surface of his work is always lively, entertaining, and instantly captivating. The minor characters who appear just once are vivid cameos because they represent what interests the director most in life: its oddities and little incongruities.

With figures like Antoine Doinel, Charlie Kohler in *Tirez sur le Pianiste,* and Pierre Lachenay in *La Peau Douce* Truffaut has created a distinctive and appealing kind of hero, a man who is diffident, sensitive, a born loser in life's battles but able to give and receive love. The films in which these characters appear have their own ethos: they show the disruptive effect of social pressures on human relationships and the overwhelming importance of love and friendship. The affection and insight Truffaut brings to them ranks him firmly in the tradition of Jean Renoir and Jacques Becker. The ideal forms for this kind of approach are loose episodic structures that allow room for spontaneity and improvisation, jokes and asides, and it is here that Truffaut makes his most significant contribution to the French cinema. In this respect too he is furthest removed from the normal image of the *avant-garde* modern director obsessed with the quest for new narrative forms and with his own creativity. There is little that is experimental in Truffaut but instead a whole dimension of charm and nostalgia, typified by his use of a Charles Trenet song and shots of the Eiffel tower to set the tone of *Baisers Volés*. In a cinema increasingly dominated by technique and intellectual complexity Truffaut offers a welcome breath of fresh air.

Should Films Be Politically Committed?
by FRANÇOIS TRUFFAUT

Why did you make this film? What relation does it have to you? How are you attached to it?

It's a film that singularly lacks any *raison d'être* . . . in the exact sense that one couldn't make the same charge about my first film, *The 400 Blows.*

When I made *The 400 Blows* I economized on the filmstock, the lighting, and the studio time because I had no reason to think it would be a commercial success. I was very conscious about that: I was making a little French film on the same scale as Leenhardt's *Les Dernières Vacances,* Lucot's *Les Dieux du Dimanche,* Riera's *La Grande Vie,* or Wheeler's *Les Premières Armes.* It was, therefore, a little French film that was neither erotic nor a detective story, likeable and gently encouraged by the press, but a film that people wouldn't go see. The success of *The 400 Blows* was a total surprise for me and I attribute it to a series of extraordinary coincidences: its selection for the Cannes Festival (what would have happened to the film if it had been finished in November of the preceding year?), the birth of the New Wave (I benefited from *The Lovers, Hiroshima, The Cousins*), that year's crisis in French production, etc. I therefore saw this modest family enterprise suddenly

Translated from "Questions à l'auteur," Cinéma 61, no. 52 (January 1971): 7–11. Copyright © 1961 by La Fédération Française des Ciné-Clubs. Reprinted by permission of Cinéma 61. Title supplied. This selection is an extract from a discussion that followed the showing of Shoot the Piano Player to members of the French Federation of Ciné-Clubs.

become a great international film that was picked up by all sorts of associations, groups, organizers of galas—how could I know?

The film escaped from my hands and became something academic that I didn't recognize anymore.

It belonged to a public that doesn't like movies, to the spectator who goes to the movies twice a year, the public of René Clair and *Bridge on the River Kwai* which I dread most in the world. With my second film I felt myself being watched, waited for by this public, and I really wanted to send them all packing. I had a number of projects for films with children; I put them all aside since I didn't want to seem to be exploiting a trick that worked well before. This time I wanted to please the real film nuts and them alone, while leading astray a large part of those who liked *The 400 Blows*. Maybe everybody was led astray by the piano player, but so much the worse.

I refused to be a prisoner of my first success. I discarded the temptation to renew that success by choosing a 'great subject.' I turned my back on what everyone waited for and I took *my pleasure* as my only rule of conduct. You won't find any exposition scene in *Piano Player* (nothing useful: everything is there for my pleasure as a filmmaker and I hope for your pleasure as a spectator).

I was free as a breeze. Therefore I chose some limit so that I wouldn't go crazy. I put myself in the position of a filmmaker who had orders imposed on him: a detective novel, American, that was to be transposed to France. Nevertheless, I chose *Shoot the Piano Player* because I admired the author, David Goodis; perhaps you movie lovers know his novel *Nightmare,* which became *Dark Passage* on the screen, directed by Delmer Daves and starring Humphrey Bogart and Lauren Bacall, or *Le Casse,* which Paul Wendkos made into a film called *The Burglar* with Jayne Mansfield and Dan Duryea. Ever since I saw *La Tête contre les murs,* I wanted to make a film with Aznavour; now I could reconcile two dreams by uniting Goodis and Aznavour.

I know that the result seems ill-assorted and the film seems to contain four or five films, but that's what I wanted. Above all I was looking for the explosion of a genre (the detective film) by mixing genres (comedy, drama, melodrama, the psychological film, the thriller, the love film, etc.). I know that the public detests

nothing more than changes in tone, but I've always had a passion
for changing tone. The shot I like best in *Zazie* is Albertine's tears.
But I do think that there's a coherence in *Piano Player:* love. In
the film men talk only about women and women talk only about
men; in the most strenuous brawls, settlings of accounts, kidnapping,
pursuits, everyone talks only about love: sexual, sentimental, physical, moral, social, marital, extramarital, etc.

In spite of the burlesque side to certain scenes, it's never a parody
(because I detest parody except when it begins to rival the beauty
of what it's parodying). For me it's something very precise that I
would call a *respectful pastiche* of the Hollywood B-films from
which I learned so much.

*Infancy isn't the only subject. Why avoid the great problems
of our time? You could always stay a film critic!*

You can say my film's useless, a failure, nothing, anything you
want, but I don't recognize your right to tell me that I ought to
make another film in its place, or treat this or that subject. You have
to judge the film I show you, that's all. I hate the kind of articles
that are appearing more and more in the newspapers, which totally condemn various films of the New Wave because of the themes
they've treated. The great problems of our time? I don't know the
answers to them; many more intelligent, cultivated, and able people than I have broken their heads on these things you want me to
mix into. I'm talking only about the things I know or I think I
know. In point of fact I could undertake a film about the Algerian
war when I want. But I don't want to, because the reality of it is
too complex for me and I could only make a negative film, a purely
negative film that would add to the confusion. Apart from Algeria
I'm also interested in Hitler, in the concentration camps, and in
racism; I read all the books that come out on those subjects. When
a journalist asks why don't the young filmmakers make a film about
Algeria, I'd like to answer: "Why don't you write a book about
Algeria? Because you wouldn't know what to write? O.K., imagine
that I wouldn't know what to film!"

Deportation fascinates me. How you get deported isn't complicated; what's strange is how you become a "deporter," how and
why *everyone* can find it normal to deport or to see other people
deported. I've read so many books about the camps that it seems

to me that I could make a film about them. But I think for a minute: what's a deportee? A sixty-six pound man. Look, sixty-six-pound characters can't act; to select skinny walk-ons as in *Le Bal des Maudits* is pure infamy. The margin of cheating between a skinny walk-on and a deportee is blasphemous and unacceptable. A documentary film is the only solution, and there Resnais has made *the* film that it was necessary to make, the only one possible, the greatest film I have ever seen. Some imbecile wrote that *The 400 Blows* was a film against secular schools because the teacher was overridden by the events. If I had been raised by the Jesuits, I would have been given the "Laic Office Prize," if it existed.

Let me tell you of my contempt for certain 'great subjects.' For me, Stanley Kramer is an outrageous schemer and his films, *The Defiant Ones* or the other about the atomic bomb, are the work of an ass. Can a white love a black and vice versa? Don't make me laugh! The person who treats a subject like that must not be very convinced himself by the answer; if he were, he wouldn't make the film. I'll go further: to talk about things like that is indecent because talking gives the feeling that the problem exists. Naturally, if the same subject had been done by Renoir, it would interest me just the same.

One can talk about "great problems" only with a terrific sincerity, so that it really stops you from sleeping at night; it won't be decided from the outside. Autant-Lara came back from Yugoslavia where he made a film on conscientious objection (thanks to me, who proved to him that censorship didn't exist), but he will always be for me the director of *La Jument Verte* and therefore an imposter. If he wasn't an imposter, if he was an *"auteur"* of films, he would have moved away from the nobility in *La Jument Verte* and the lewdness in *L'Objecteur* because there is no noble or ignoble genre, there is no genre, I say, as *Shoot the Piano Player* proves, and I'm going to finish by praising it myself even if you spit on it.

Be logical, sir. When you reproach me for making *Piano Player* and not some great "generous" film you are reproaching me for having lacked generosity. But look, if, being what I am, what you see me to be, I had externally took on a "great subject" as your heart wants me to, I would have been insincere, since I had in my heart a sleeping *Piano Player*. Therefore, this general film that I haven't made, wouldn't it be like Kramer's horrible films that I was just talking about, international blablabla, misused cinema? Now you see I was right to make the film I made; in any case that's the one I ask you to judge and not the imaginary one that I hope I'll be able to make someday.

Uncommitted Artist?
by PENELOPE HOUSTON

Left-wing critics in this country seem to have been thrown dis-
tinctly off-balance by Truffaut's *Tirez sur le Pianiste*. No one has
had the nerve to write, though some people have said, that Truffaut
may have to be written off as a serious filmmaker if this is the way
he intends to carry on. Apparently the audience which saw the film
at a meeting of the French Federation of Ciné-Clubs towards the
end of last year shared some of these reservations. At any rate,
Cinéma 61 in its January issue published Truffaut's detailed answers to the questions asked him: answers which are revealing of
the artist's position, and not irrelevant in relation to the critic's.

The basis of these critics' dissatisfaction is nothing more or less
than a sense of let-down. *Les Quatre Cents Coups* was humanist,
engaged, autobiography with a conscience. It was also a film which
satisfied everyone, arousing instantaneous sympathy and liking. Yes,
Truffaut says rather bitterly, "I started out to make a little film,
something which the press would quietly encourage but which people wouldn't go to see. Then I saw this modest little family enterprise become a big international success . . . It belonged to the
public which has no affection for the cinema, to the man who goes
to the pictures once a year to see *Bridge on the River Kwai* or the
new Clair film, the public I mistrust most in the world." And so:
"This time I wanted to please only the real enthusiasts . . . and my
only rule in making *Tirez sur le Pianiste* was my own pleasure . . .

From "Critic's Notebook," Sight and Sound *30, no. 2 (Spring 1961):*
64–65. Copyright © 1961 by Sight and Sound. *Reprinted by permis-*
sion of Sight and Sound *and the author.*

I would call the film a respectful pastiche of the Hollywood B-film, from which I have learnt such a lot."

"I know," Truffaut says, "that there is nothing the public dislikes more than abrupt changes of mood, but I have always loved them . . ." Practically speaking, the remarkable thing is that he was able to carry out this disregard for audience tastes, to make the film as he wanted. And what did he want to make? A record, almost, of a love affair with the cinema, a film full of jokes and allusions and tricks and charm. Godard's dedication of *À Bout de Souffle* "to Monogram Pictures" and Truffaut's avowed desire to do a pastiche of the B-picture are very personal variations on the French intellectuals' passionate attachment to a dream America. Truffaut has clearly haunted the cinema since his childhood. *Tirez sur le Pianiste* exists so much in the context of other films that you feel anyone who hasn't followed at least something of his own route to it could only be mystified.

To be pompous about a film like this, treating its director like a youth club leader who has been caught carrying a flick-knife, is merely trying to dragoon the artist into one's own camp. He has no intention of being pinned down, as his film makes sufficiently clear. His answer to the second question asked him—"why dodge the big issues of our time?"—is even more specific.

"You can," he says, "find my film useless, a misfire, a negation, anything you like. What I don't accept is your right to tell me that I ought to have been making something else instead . . . When a journalist asks me 'Why aren't young filmmakers doing pictures about Algeria?' what I'd like to answer is 'Why don't you write a book about Algeria?' Because you wouldn't know just what to write? Well, then, I wouldn't know what to film!" He goes on to attack the Stanley Kramer type of problem picture, with its holier than thou self-righteousness, its lack of urgency or desperate conviction. "You can only," he says, "talk of the 'big problems' with devastating sincerity if they really keep you from sleeping at night." And consequently: "If, being what I am, I had tackled one of these 'big subjects' you want me to film, approaching it from the outside, I would have been dishonest since there would still have been in my heart a sleeping *Pianist* . . ."

One's sympathies are all on Truffaut's side. This is the way an artist functions; and for the critic to stand on the sidelines and try to shout the players down is not only futile but mannerless. Truffaut has chosen an obvious example to quote against his critics: films like Kramer's *The Defiant Ones* and *On the Beach*, so respectable, so genuinely well-meaning, so unassailably correct, are empty precisely because the sense of involvement at a personal level is missing. The element of evasive smugness in the social conscience film has itself become a cliché, from Kazan's *Pinky*, which made it easy to sympathize with its Negro heroine because, after all, she was really Jeanne Crain, to Guy Green's *The Mark*, which appeals for a more tolerant attitude to sex criminals but won't take the risk of making its hero guilty of anything more substantial than an impulse.

All the same, Truffaut is really taking us down a false trail. No one expects the filmmaker dutifully to sit down with a list of "big subjects" and tick them off one by one. What one could say is that his understandable retreat from the intimidating difficulty of the social subjects needn't lead him all the way to a private fantasy world of his own. We can't, again, presume to tell him that he ought to be concerned with some aspect of social reality; but we can ask why he isn't, what is the condition of the society he's living in which makes him so unwilling to come to grips with it. *Tirez sur le Pianiste* is almost a classic example of the kind of work John Berger means, I think, in the quotation I've used earlier in these notes. To enjoy it fully you must "accept what the artist himself is trying to do . . . that it is necessary for him to create a kind of tidal world of flux . . ."

It isn't very difficult to do this: to enjoy the mixture of character study, gangster fantasy, comedy and pathos; to take Truffaut's film precisely at his own evaluation of it and to recognize the honesty as well as the impudence which has gone into its making. It throws off sparks like a Catherine-wheel, a fizzing, dazzling, short-lived divertissement. It comes not from an uncommitted artist, but from an artist who recognises in himself the necessity to be committed all the way. And his emphasis on the difficulty (the emotional, rather than the economic problem) of this is something on which critics of the left might usefully comment.

Improvisation in Film-Acting:
An Interview with Albert Finney
and Mary Ure
by LOUIS MARCORELLES

Marcorelles: Do you think film directors pay enough attention
to the actor? Do they give you time to prepare your part and
achieve the kind of concentration you want?

Ure: I don't really think so. I've only done five films so far, and
of course I don't know how they work in Europe. But I think the
best thing would be to have a group of actors improvise round
scenes, get to know each other, and then work the film through.
That could be exciting.

Finney: Preparation's essential. Making a film involves such a
long period of creation, and in theory at least the first day's shooting
is intended to be part of the finished film. So it's important, even
on the first day, that you should all know what you're aiming at.
Of course you're bound to find out more about the subject as you
work, but the more preparation you can do beforehand the better
it is for everyone.

Ure: But you ought not to work on the scenes themselves. I'd
like to work round them, to get to know how the other actors and
the director work, to get a feeling of everybody's attitude to the

*Exerpted from "Albert Finney and Mary Ure Talking about Acting,"
by Louis Marcorelles,* Sight and Sound *30, no. 2 (Spring 1961): 57–58.
Reprinted by permission of* Sight and Sound *and the author. Title
supplied.*

film. If you work too hard on a scene, though, I find the vitality just goes—at least it does for me.

Finney: Well, it doesn't for me because I like to know just what I want to achieve with a scene. I want the dress rehearsal, if you like, of a shot in a film to be as perfect as possible technically, and then when we're actually shooting it I like to be able to forget that side altogether. But in filming they never seem to rehearse enough: they're not that interested, so they treat it as a sort of joke.

Ure: But you can overrehearse.

Finney: Well, of course. It's a question of balance: all art is, in any case. At the moment—I like to say at the moment, because I never know when my ideas may change—I believe very strongly in form. Improvisation can be dangerous, and I felt that about *Shadows.* After all, if you want to make a film about a certain subject you must also want certain things to emerge; and you can't just leave it to chance that those things are going to emerge in the right balance.

Marcorelles: You get a good deal of improvisation in a film like Truffaut's *Tirez sur la Pianiste.* He wants his actors to show their characters through their nerves and their physical reactions as much as their dialogue, and he's not particularly strict about his text. What do you feel about this?

Ure: I think it works. I felt *Tirez sur le Pianiste* was a remarkable personal statement, which every great film has to be; and it gave me the feeling of a progression in the cinema, some kind of advance.

Finney: I agree that Truffaut's feeling about his subject emerges very strongly, and of course this is what should happen. You ought to feel that the director is cajoling you, or bullying you, or seducing you into his attitude. At the same time, the conception of some of the performances seemed a bit untidy: they didn't communicate to me, and I felt that perhaps because of this freedom and improvisation they weren't always certain about just what they *meant* to communicate.

Ure: But it was such a relief to find a film that didn't give you everything on a plate, all neatly worked out with a beginning and a middle and an end, and all technically perfect . . . You don't sense that Truffaut has a cameraman saying "You can't do *that;*

it's too difficult," and a producer saying "You can't shoot *that*; it'll be too expensive." You feel he does exactly what he wants; and if we had more directors in England who were in love with their subjects, and who felt that they had this kind of personal freedom, I think our cinema would be a very different thing.

Marcorelles: In fact Truffaut's film was shot entirely outside the studio, on a small budget and with complete freedom. I was there, for instance, when he did one of the scenes between Aznavour and Nicole Berger, and he was alone with just the two actors and the cameraman.

Ure: Well, of course, that's wonderful. And it's an enormous help to be in a real location. When we were doing the last scene in *Look Back in Anger*—the scene at the railway station where I meet Jimmy Porter again—we shot it at four o'clock in the morning and we did it in a single take. We couldn't possibly have managed that in a studio, without the help we got from the atmosphere, the smoke and the rain and the way the station felt.

Finney: In *Saturday Night and Sunday Morning* I felt like that about the scenes where I was working at the lathe. I felt almost like a sculptor—working a real lathe, with real metal, and working it myself. It's wonderful for an actor to be able to pour his concentration into an actual object like this, until in a way it becomes part of him. I found that one of the most exciting things about filming.

Marcorelles: I'd like here to bring in Brecht and the so-called Brechtian attitude, which means that you are very conscious about what you are doing and why you're doing it and also involves a certain sense of distance—the opposite, in a way, from Truffaut's method. Do you think this is just a matter of theory, or does it mean something for you in practical terms?

Finney: Well, I'm very consciously trying, as an actor, to keep myself free from theories. I'm very much concerned with the particular way I'm growing, with the way I think one thing one week and another thing next week. Of course I'm interested to read about theories, but I'm not too anxious to adopt them or become too engrossed in them . . . The process of the emotional and mental growth of a part ought to combine very closely with the technical growth, and if one wants to communicate a certain effect or feeling, one has got in rehearsals to try to find the clearest way to achieve that cleanly. If you can manage that sort of perfection in rehearsal, then when you actually get in front of an audience, or when the cameras are rolling, you can give it the breath of life in the actual performing of it.

Ure: I agree that it's essential for an actor to have read widely about all kinds of theories, but it's just as important for him to be adaptable. He ought at a moment's notice to be able to work in a completely different way because that's what an exciting director wants him to do. Perhaps a Brechtian director doesn't believe there *is* any other way.

Marcorelles: You believe more in the kind of chance happening which may come up during the actual shooting.

Ure: Of course it's important to rehearse properly, to know what you're doing in a scene. But in the cinema—and this is one of the reasons why I find such excitement in films—there is always the chance that something in a shot may go slightly wrong; and in that case you need this little bit of freedom just to give something truly creative. Surely this chance thing is terribly important: some of the best things in the cinema have come about by chance.

Finney: But if something goes wrong and you have to cope, for want of a better word, you can cope in a way which is good for the film or one which is bad for the film. Even if I'd only dropped a cup and saucer, for instance, I'd like to feel that the way I pick it up would be influenced by the fact that I was in the right rhythm of the scene.

From an Interview
with FRANÇOIS TRUFFAUT

In one sense, I made *Shoot the Piano Player* in reaction to *The 400 Blows,* because the success of the film, the imbalance that I suddenly discovered [between the sympathy accorded the child and the antagonism toward the parents], so flabbergasted me that I said to myself: "I must pay attention, I must not fall into demagoguery." But I don't really understand very well what happened in *Piano Player.* In the final analysis, I had to be too faithful to the book. I was too sure of myself, because of the success of *The 400 Blows.* But I think that's a law of the second film. Thus, *A Woman Is a Woman* (because *Le Petit Soldat* was banned, I consider the other to be Godard's second film) is done in the euphoria of *Breathless. Vivre sa Vie* is a complete recovery.

In a first film, you take the plunge: let's go, I'm risking everything; after this I may not make any more films, but for now I want to see how this will turn out. The reaction to the first film is very important. If it succeeds, one is always astonished. The second shows this. *Marienbad* too shows a great self-confidence, born of an unexpected success. All these second films have this in common: they are less complete than the first in which there was a whole beginning of life to express, when you wanted to say everything. The second film becomes intentionally more modest in de-

*Excerpted and translated from "Entretien avec François Truffaut," *Cahiers du Cinéma, no. 138 (December 1962): 49–51. Copyright © 1962 by Les Editions de l'Etoile. Reprinted by permission of Les Editions de l'Etoile and Grove Press, Inc. Title supplied.*

sign. It's the third that's the most interesting: it's a reflection on what happened in the other two and marks the start of a career.

If you think about *Piano Player,* you see that the scenario doesn't stand up under analysis. It really lacks a directing idea. There is a directing idea in both my other films. In *The 400 Blows,* it's a question of presenting as honestly as possible a child who has been guided by a moral stand. The same goes for *Jules and Jim:* if you did it this way, it would be porno; like this, indelicate; like this, conventional; so it's necessary to make it in a different way. The mistake in *Piano Player* is that you can do anything with it; it's material whose form doesn't impose itself. Aznavour has terrific comic power: I could have made a comic film. He has great authority: the character could have been ferocious. At the start I didn't have any set purpose, only a crazy desire to use Aznavour, because of *La Tête contre les murs;* but it would have been better if I had known him for a long time. The really courageous thing I've done in *Piano Player* is to use flashbacks, while knowing that they are never forgiven. I said to Braunberger: Remember *Les Mauvais Rencontres?* And *Lola Montès?* And *The Barefoot Contessa?* Those didn't work because of the flashbacks. Well, we'll treat ourselves to two of them, one inside the other. In fact, that throws everything up in the air.

It's a law: you can't mix things up. You can't be fully in one story and fully in another. If you worked at it a little, *Piano Player* could be narrated in chronological fashion. You have to work at it. There are good things in the film, but no one can say: this is the best that's been done on this theme. There is no theme.

What about this one: a man is caught in the gears of life, rejects them, and, at the end, resigns himself to them. Courage, cowardice . . . ?

Even if you accept that, there are parasitic things in the film. And also there's the director who resigns himself to entering the gears of a gangster film! I didn't think of it beforehand, but while I shot *Piano Player,* I saw that I abhorred gangster films. Now I wouldn't write laudatory articles about *Rififi.* I believe you don't have to create sympathetic gangsters, weeping truants, or set up the nice people against the nasty ones. If you do that, you get a film in which all the bourgeois conventions are transposed into the gangster world. That's why I decided to make my gangsters comic: it was the only solution if I didn't want to fall into conventionality —and I made fun of them a little. To make up for that, it was necessary that they be a little frightening, an effect I achieved through the boy's kidnapping and the death of Marie Dubois. That reawakened the people who otherwise would have believed that they were dealing with English puppets. But it's dangerous to change ideas in the course of a film. You should have an idea at the start and then strengthen it, as I did in my two other films, where the idea was originally poorly expressed in the scenario. If I had known beforehand that Aznavour and Nicole Berger would make an extraordinary couple (he worked less well with the others than with her), I would have made a film about the two of them.

Another thing must have offended the public in Piano Player: *the rupture of tone that characterizes several films that didn't work —A* Woman Is a Woman *for one—and it's something the French public has never accepted.*

Yes, that's the most difficult thing to get by. In any case people in America understand *Piano Player,* but differently; they laughed without stopping, even in the dramatic passages. The first song is comic, but they laughed all through the second, which theoretically is not.

Anyway, you can say what you like to me, but *Piano Player* still needs a month of work. Mix together two or three reels of film that you like, and you won't get a film that will interest people, even if there are good things in it. It's true that change of tone is a thing to work for; it's a gamble that has to be tried sometimes, and Renoir has succeeded in doing it.

On SHOOT
THE PIANO PLAYER
by GRAHAM PETRIE

Tirez sur le Pianiste (*Shoot the Pianist/Shoot the Piano Player*) is a gangster story that refuses to behave like a gangster story, a love story that refuses to behave like a love story, a film that refuses to conform to our assumptions about what a film can and should do. Its unsettling and disorienting quality, however, comes less from unusual or experimental camera techniques than from bizarre and unexpected juxtapositions of mood, setting, and action, from constant and sudden alternations between farce and tragedy, and from the nature and behavior of the characters involved. The tone is established in the opening sequence, which presents us with the totally unexplained situation of a man fleeing from unseen pursuers (represented only by the sound and headlights of their car). We are forced into automatic identification with him, partly by his situation, and partly through repeated close-ups of his anxious, hunted face. While we are busy on the intellectual level trying to work out the mystery of the situation, we are further unsettled visually by the circumstances of the filming: normally a night scene of this kind, even if shot (like this one) in real streets, would be artificially lit in such a way that we could follow the

From The Cinema of François Truffaut *by Graham Petrie, (New York: A. S. Barnes & Co., 1970), pp. 23–27, 82–85, 119–21, 127, 143–44, 148, 161–64, 176. Copyright © 1970 by A. S. Barnes & Co. Reprinted by permission of A. S. Barnes & Co. and The Tantivy Press. Title supplied.*

characters clearly. Here, however, only available light is used, with the result that Chico (the man being chased) moves abruptly and disconcertingly from the full glare of a streetlamp into complete darkness, then back into half-light again, and into shots of this kind are intercut jarring flashes of the headlights of the pursuing car. A sudden long shot abruptly distances us from Chico: we see him stumble and hurtle, in almost comic fashion, into a lamppost; laughter at the awkwardness of his fall is stifled by our realization that he seems to be hurt. He lies there moaning, we hear footsteps, we see someone bend over him ominously and slap his face. The newcomer helps him up; we expect him to be an enemy and are prepared for violence, but Chico simply brushes himself off, thanks him, and the two walk off together like old friends. They begin a conversation which quickly takes a very personal turn and Chico's helper takes the opportunity to tell a perfect stranger details of his private life which he could tell no one else. He talks about love, sex, the disillusionments and compensations of marriage as they walk on through patches of light and darkness, his voice competing with the sound of their footsteps and the roar of traffic. They stop at a corner and say goodbye, the other leaves, Chico looks round and abruptly begins to run again—we are suddenly reminded that the danger to him was neither imaginary nor forgotten.

Almost every feature of this sequence is designed to disorient the audience: Raoul Coutard's deliberately rough camera style, the lighting (or lack of it), the total absence of background music that might help the audience to develop an appropriate emotional response, and especially the confusion as to whether and when we should experience fear, relief, or laughter, and to what extent we are intended to identify with the characters. This uncertainty continues throughout the film: in the sequence that follows in the bar where Charlie works, the violence of the gangsters' pursuit of Chico and Charlie's intervention to foil them is followed by the inanity of the waiter's ridiculous song—ridiculous both in its nonsense words and the jerky, puppetlike movements of the singer (yet the words, emphasizing the incongruity of sexual relationships, relate to a major theme of the film). Other scenes inside the bar have a strange, unsettling quality—Chico seizes, dances with, and propositions the barman's mistress all within the space of a couple of minutes; Charlie's prostitute girl friend is seen conducting a strange dance with a young man in which she lures him to her then pushes him contemptuously away, finally provoking him to violence; we are given brief glimpses of background conversations about sex and of tentative sexual advances between people dancing. All these scenes are thematically viable, but the way in which they are presented causes us to start questioning actions and responses we had previously taken for granted.

The film is full of incidents where serious actions are shot in a comic way: Charlie is abducted by having a quite monstrous gun pointed at his nose in the middle of the street and Lena is bustled into the gangsters' car while passersby look calmly on (this scene may well have been shot with a hidden camera); once in the car, however, captors and captured get on well together, joke and reminisce about their childhood. This approach is crystallized in the scene of the killing of the barman, which begins with the quarrel between Lena and the barman, from which Charlie attempts to remain detached, but which reaches a pitch of virulence that forces him to intervene. A ridiculous yet potentially dangerous duel of telephone receiver against carving knife follows, the absurdity of it being heightened by wildly overemphatic music; Charlie chases his opponent outside but throws down his knife and attempts reconciliation; there is a moment of relief and exhaustion, till the apparently friendly gesture by the barman of putting his arm round Charlie's shoulder turns into attempted murder as he tries to choke him. This scene is shot in dispassionate close-up as the expressionless barman talks (as does every character in the film once given the opportunity) of his life history and the misery of his sex life, while Charlie gasps helplessly for breath beside him. Then comes the struggle for possession of the knife and the ambiguous stabbing, in which Charlie seems to use rather more force that he later claims he did or intended to. In this scene, as almost everywhere else in the film, camera virtuosity is secondary to abrupt changes of mood established by cutting or juxtaposition within the frame, together with brusque transitions in place and action. The two most pervasive stylistic features—the handheld camera and the relentless use of available light, which often leaves the screen in near-complete darkness (elements which are combined in the long sequence of Charlie's arrival at the farm and walk up the hillside with his brother Richard)—create a deliberate visual roughness, a lack of normal technical polish, that by breaking down our stylistic preconceptions about film, enable us to accept more readily this world where farce, sadness, violence, death, and laughter clash and coincide. We are not, of course, being shown a new world; we are simply seeing our own world, as though for the first time, with unprecedented spontaneity, freshness, and vitality. By breaking down our accepted notions of cause and effect, by destroying our normal expectations and assumptions about pattern and order and neat categorization of experience, Truffaut has given us a means of apprehending the real world around us more intelligently and perceptively, for it is the real world he has shown us.

There are some occasions in *Tirez sur le Pianiste,* particularly in the love scenes, where the camera is allowed to take on the kind of creative function characteristic of *Jules and Jim.* In the early scene between Charlie and Clarisse (the prostitute) a mood of purely sensuous and physical pleasure predominates, an atmosphere of almost routine yet still enjoyable behavior. There is something ritualistic about the spatial detachment and separation of the lovers: Charlie lies in bed watching Clarisse undress and, despite (or perhaps because of) their obvious long familiarity with each other, she feels the need to titillate and stimulate him with a kind of striptease performance, hiding behind a screen and displaying piece by piece each segment of her seductive black underwear. (Characteristically for this film, having waved her black panties at him, she proceeds to emerge unexpectedly wearing her slip.) The sense of voyeurism is heightened by the way in which the camera pans to follow her, as though through Charlie's eyes, as she moves about the room. Finally she emerges nude (the uncut version of the film pokes fun at both the censor and the voyeuristic instincts of the audience by including a shot in which she is allowed to expose her breasts and Charlie immediately covers them with a sheet, telling her that the censor wouldn't approve). With an expression of comical lust on his face Charlie proceeds to wind up his alarm clock, put out the light, and dive under the sheets with her, to the accompaniment of muffled squeals on her part. The effect of the whole scene is external, detached; there is a sense of welcome physical enjoyment but little or no emotional commitment—the impression of a performance or a routine (heightened by brief shots of Charlie's metronome and by the reference to the censor) is strong . . .

The two flashback love scenes between Charlie and his wife have a quality of tension and false reconciliation. In the quarrel scene, as Theresa tries to tell him how much he has changed, the camera pans to and fro angrily with Charlie, then a close-up of his face turns out disconcertingly to be a mirror shot, the camera moves to bring her "real" presence into frame while he remains a reflection, finally both become briefly "real" as reconciliation is reached and a gentle pan accompanies them as they relax onto the bed. The fragility and misunderstandings of the relationship are conveyed vividly through the camera movements and the framing. In the later scene where Theresa confesses her affair with the impresario Schmeel, the camera follows her as she wanders round the room desperately trying to explain, close-ups of her face against a blank white background emphasize her isolation, and a close-up catches Charlie's indecision as he tells himself to go to her and help her but inevitably makes the wrong decision and leaves.

In contrast to the scenes with Clarisse and Theresa, the one physical and detached, the camera content merely to observe, the other emotional and involving as the camera forces us into proximity with the characters, the love scene with Lena is both remote and immediate, serene and unsettling. After the flashback to Charlie's earlier career, the camera returns to the poster of him as Edouard Saroyan the pianist on Lena's bedroom wall, then pans slowly round the room taking in furniture, ornaments, discarded clothing; a close-up of Lena and Charlie kissing is superimposed on this, then vanishes as the shot ends on the two of them in bed. Lena is talking to him, he is passive, perhaps not even listening; brief dissolves to shots of the lovers together at earlier or later stages of the night punctuate her speech, revealing a wonderfully beautiful rhythm in themselves, but also creating a sense of fragmentation and separateness, a fragile and lovely harmony, never staying constant for long and always on the brink of disruption. The essential isolation of the lovers, the inability of the one truly to reach the other, is ironically counterpointed in the scene of Lena's death at the end of the film, as she slides in a breathtakingly beautiful sweep down a bank of snow and Charlie and Fido stumble towards her body. All Charlie can do on reaching her is to brush the snow and blood from her face; a zoom into her now totally alien and un-reachable beauty underlines his loss, yet a dissolve to the face of the new barmaid as he returns to work prepares us for the beginning of a new cycle of hesitation, commitment too late, destruction, and loss.

The film is also full of visual devices and jokes, some of them bringing dead metaphors unexpectedly to life: the "two-faced" barman is shown betraying Charlie and Lena in a split-screen shot that catches him in three different postures; one of the gangsters pleads for his mother to drop dead if he is lying and, framed in an antique oval design, an old lady clutches her heart and falls flat on her back, large, clumping boots rising and subsiding as her body hits the floor. The arbitrariness of normal screen conventions and continuity is indicated as Lena holds up a mirror to show Charlie the gangsters following several yards behind them in the street— and their faces loom huge and overwhelming on the screen. Throughout *Tirez sur le Pianiste* Truffaut presents us with a con-stant tension between spontaneity and stylization, between what we expect and what we actually see on the screen; and the incongruous rhythms and bizarre juxtapositions force a continual process of re-adjustment on the viewer as he watches, yet leave him at the end free to make his own application of what he has experienced . . .

The world of the "present tense" of the film creates a closed en-vironment from which Charlie has to escape physically if he is to redeem himself. At first sight the world created in the flashback seems to offer a deliberate contrast in sophistication and glamor, yet visually the two settings have a great deal in common. Charlie's world of fame and fortune is constricting and enclosed; it has an almost unreal quality about it, created largely through the lighting. Almost all the scenes in this section of the film are interiors—café, hotel room, audition, concert hall, press conference, the office where Lars Schmeel the impresario talks to Charlie/Edouard about his future (the lighting in this scene making the city seen through the office window look totally unreal). The implication rises inevitably from this that even in his "good" times Charlie moves in a world of his own and never really relates to other people. Even as a success-ful pianist he uses the piano as a barrier behind which he shelters or hides—an idea vividly conveyed in a shot which has the piano cover two-thirds of the screen with Charlie's expressionless face squeezed into the triangle left in the top right-hand corner.

The use of corridors in the flashback sequence increases the sense of unease that the other elements of this part of the film convey, and intensifies the feeling of a closed environment with no discerni-ble exit for the characters. The most effective scene in this respect shows Charlie on his way to his audition, moving uneasily along a seemingly endless corridor. He walks in a jerky, hunched-up, almost uncoordinated way, wearing a coat much too large for him into which we feel he will vanish the moment things begin to get difficult and he needs to escape. He looks pathetic, comic, and vulnerable, all at once, and the hand held camera that tracks back in front of him, tilting and rocking the frame slightly as it moves, crystallizes these essential elements in him. When he at last summons up enough courage to ring the bell and enters the room he is replaced by a girl carrying a violin who begins to walk away from the door down the corridor. The camera unexpectedly chooses to follow her rather than Charlie; it tracks smoothly away in front of her and we hear Charlie strike the first few confident notes on the piano. Still we accompany the girl, however; her face is tense and strained, she clutches her violin tightly and awkwardly, and a sense of unease and puzzlement is created at the time we should be sharing Charlie's apparent triumph. There is a cut; we expect at last to join Charlie, but instead we see the girl again, crossing a courtyard with buildings surrounding her on all sides. She stops and looks upwards as, totally unnaturalistically, the sound of Charlie's playing swells louder around her. By filming the turning point of Charlie's career in this way, Truffaut creates a vivid sense of how fragile and temporary the *façade* which he is creating will turn out to be . . .

The city in *Tirez sur le Pianiste* is balanced by nature to some extent at the end, but here too Truffaut refuses to romanticize the countryside. Nature is cold and neutral, the cottage the Saroyans are hiding in is squatly and almost absurdly isolated. The approach to the hideout is shot so that the countryside itself is rarely seen: with the two gangsters focus is placed almost entirely on the interior of the car and their conversation with Fido; with Charlie and Lena, Truffaut and Raoul Coutard create an almost abstract pattern of streetlights and then falling snow on the smeared windshield. Nature of course provides no escape: Lena is shot and left to die in the snow; Charlie reaches her too late and can do nothing except brush blood and clinging snow from her face. The two sets of crooks exit in a farcical chase to continue their meaningless and absurd hostility, and Charlie is left back almost exactly where he started . . .

Though I personally find the music of *Les 400 Coups* satisfactory in its creation of a sense of lyricism in the grubby back streets of Paris and its involvement of the audience in Antoine's experiences, it is possible for an unsympathetic viewer to find it closer to the traditional emotional conditioning of the audience than that of any other of Truffaut's films. Jean Constantin's music for *Tirez sur le Pianiste,* however, is required to serve totally different purposes and the result is a score almost as subtle and as essential to the final impact of the film as that of *Jules et Jim.* Much of the sound in the film is "natural," in the sense that it consists of music played by Charlie as part of his daily work (this device is used in *L'Amour à Vingt Ans* where virtually all the music consists of the classical music Antoine hears at concerts, plays in the record shop he works in, or listens to on his record player). Charlie is identified from the beginning with one particular tune, one he knows so well that he can play it without thinking, just as he tries to lead a life so centered round routine and mechanical repetition of the same experiences that he will no longer need to think or feel about anything. In the scenes in the bar at the beginning of the film we see other ways in which music can be used to deaden, avoid, or smooth over unexpected emotional eruptions. After the fracas with the gangsters and their pursuit of Chico, the waiter's song immediately establishes order and routine and the customers forget the incident at once, while throughout these scenes the incessant slickness of the dance music provides a background to an astonishing variety of sexual advances—which, because of the background, are taken for granted and unresented.

The first "unnatural" music in the film establishes the basic love theme as Charlie and Lena walk home from the bar, but background music as such is relatively sparse. The love theme, generally restrained and subdued like that of *La Peau Douce,* undegoes the same kind of process as the closing music of *Les 400 Coups,* rising to a note of anguished finality and abruptness as the camera zooms in on Lena's face as she lies dead in the snow. Elsewhere music is used for scenes of violent activity like Charlie's fight with the barman and the final shoot-out at the farm, for moments of suspense and waiting, to cover transitions, and in the major love scenes—with Clarisse, the sound of a radio from next door (suggesting perhaps the mechanical nature of the relationship); with Theresa, "their" love theme; with Lena, Charlie's piano tune orchestrated so that it is both different and recognizable, just as his love for Lena has only superficially affected his general outlook on life. But the main originality of the music rests in the way in which the virtual identity of Charlie and his piano is conveyed throughout. The flashback to his days as a concert pianist is introduced by the normal piano theme modulating into a piece of classical music; it ends with Charlie's circling round the piano in the bar, sitting down, and striking a few resounding concertlike blows while a dissolve covers an almost automatic and inevitable drift into the tune that is to provide his identity, his shell, and his armor for the rest of his life. Later, as Lena and the barman quarrel, he wanders over to the piano and tinkles a few notes on it before making his one belated and disastrous attempt to become involved with something outside himself. And at the end he briefly tries out a new tune before slipping, unconsciously and inexorably, into the routine he can never again escape from . . .[1]

In *Tirez sur le Pianiste* the two songs heard in the bar at the beginning of the film both deal with sex as a crudely pleasurable physical activity in much the same way as most of the conversations and actions in the first half of the film do, and as Charlie would like to be able to and thus avoid the complications of giving himself emotionally. The second song in particular, with its breathless

[1] Some North American prints of the film crudely overemphasize Charlie's impasse by a voice-over repetition here of the barman's earlier "Music is what we need, man!" which is not in the original French prints.

succession of apparent nonsense words (flashed out on the screen even in the French version to reassure audiences that they are hearing what they think they are) catches perfectly the tone and mood of the visual side of the film, with, in both cases, serious implications hidden underneath. Later in the film, the song Charlie and Lena hear on the car radio as they drive to the farm (the words continuous over a series of dissolves in space and time) takes up the themes of loyalty, betrayal, and emotional honesty that are on the point of working themselves out . . .

Charlie Koller's series of interior monologues in *Tirez sur le Pianiste* has something of the effect of a narrator explaining his thoughts, but it is really much closer to the kind of incessant inner conversation that we all carry on with ourselves almost every waking minute. It expresses very forcefully the essential conflict between the two aspects of Charlie's personality, summing up his fears, hopes, regrets, desires, and good intentions, together with his inability to do anything about them at the right time. He is constantly addressing himself in questions or imperatives, asking what he should do or desperately trying to order himself into action. There is only one occasion where the promptings of his actual behavior coincide: after Chico has fled from the bar pursued by the gangsters, Charlie tells himself not to get involved and simply "say good luck to him," following this with a muttered "Bonne chance!" aloud. But where the inner voice recommends involvement Charlie does his best not to listen and, if he does act, does so half-heartedly and too late. The result is not always as tragic as when he tells himself to forgive and comfort his wife when she confesses her infidelity, but yields instead to jealousy and inertia, leaves, changes his mind and returns to find her dead. Walking along the street with Lena he holds an anguished debate as to whether to try to hold her hand, attempts fumblingly to do so and is repulsed, then rehearses various elegant and sophisticated ways of asking her to have a drink with him before blurting out "D'ya want a drink?" only to find that she has vanished (a scene that reminds me irresistibly of Charlie Brown trying to think of the right words with which to present his Valentine to the little red-haired girl and doing so finally with a confident "Happy Christmas!" Both Charlies possess a common inability to make their inner and outer worlds coincide or even come within touching distance). The final metamorphosis of the inner voice ironically reverses the normal process as Charlie sits at his piano during the quarrel in the bar telling himself to stay out of it and suddenly finds himself taking part after all.

The dualities of Charlie's nature and of the world he moves in are echoed in the dialogue elsewhere in the film. The language of most of the characters is extremely slangy, down-to-earth, full of sexual jokes and innuendoes, reflecting Charlie's desire to punish himself by forcing himself into as sordid an environment as he can stand and systematically debasing or ignoring the values he had lived by previously. Conversations are short and terse, and Charlie himself speaks as little and as briefly as possible. He chooses to be in this environment but can never be fully part of it, as we see in the conversation in the car with the gangsters where Lena's smile becomes more and more knowing as the coarseness of the conversation becomes more explicit, till she finally takes an active part in it, while Charlie sits rather bewildered in the back seat and finally ventures as his contribution his father's remark that once you've seen one woman you've seen them all. The characters of this milieu are constantly attempting to explain and define themselves, but have neither the verbal nor the intellectual sophistication to succeed, though their very attempts are enough to give us insight into them. The flashback shows us a different world, where people talk more fluently and coherently, but where Charlie is equally ill at ease and uncomfortable. He can adjust fully to neither world, verbally, emotionally, or morally, and the result is the insecurity which plagues him throughout.

Charlie Koller of *Tirez sur le Pianiste* attempts like the trio of *Jules et Jim* to live apart from society, but instead of moving into a wider, freer, more vital world, he retreats into one that is even more enclosed and restricted than that of normal experience. He makes more of a conscious choice than Pierre* does, but is equally unable to commit himself firmly to one course of action. Having failed his wife in a moment of extreme crisis, he wishes to avoid hurting himself or others in the future, but chooses a method which ensures that he will go on repeating his earlier mistake rather than correcting it. He tries to withdraw from social and personal relation-

* [The hero of *La peau douce*—ED.]

ships as far as possible and maintains a *façade* of aloofness and impassivity. Yet at the same time he continues to make himself available to others by living and working in their world, assuming that they will recognize and accept the dissociation he himself makes between his private, mental world and that in which he earns his bread. (It is also perhaps a subconscious acceptance of his real need of others.) But this doesn't work; others are fascinated, puzzled, or antagonized by him and attempt to draw him out, either for their own advantage, as Chico and his brothers do, or with the aim of helping him, as Lena does. Family loyalty, gratitude, love, guilt, all of them emotions he had thought he had suppressed, combine to make him respond to their promptings, but his refusal to acknowledge the effect of these emotions on him till too late ensures that he never makes the right decision at the right time. He allows others to take the initiative for him and tries to opt out of responsibility until circumstances drag him in at a stage when he has no control over the course of events and can do nothing to prevent disaster. At the end of the film the introduction of a new barmaid and the sight of the impassive Charlie playing the same tune he has played throughout indicate that nothing has really changed for him and he will slip inexorably back into the old pattern. He shares with Jules, Jim and Catherine the assumption that his telling himself that he no longer has certain emotions will automatically dispel them, and with Pierre the belief that if he sits tight and does nothing, things will somehow work themselves out. The result is an impasse in which commitment leads inexorably to disaster and lack of commitment proves impossible.

Despite Charlie's obvious weaknesses and self-deception, and the sordid surroundings, people, and conversation in which he chooses to move, it is impossible for us either to judge him or to dissociate ourselves from him. The style of the film disorients in a way which makes us ready to look at things with a fresh eye, and mingled with the shabbiness and weariness of the characters are humor and insight; people come vividly alive with very human weaknesses, needs, disappointments, self-protective deceptions, and *façades* that in the long run don't fool anyone, least of all themselves. Charlie's mask of world-heavy impassivity is contantly being knocked aside by the interior monologue which reveals his fundamental insecurity and vulnerability. His solution to the risks of life and involvement with other people is to make himself "smaller and smaller," to retreat into a "little circle" which shuts off the outside world as far as possible. As the other characters show, this is a not uncommon device, yet it is his failure to succeed with it, his acceptance of his need and responsibility for others which, paradoxically, humanizes him, and an ability to take Charlie into the worlds we ourselves have created and to accept our affinity with him can humanize us.

Truffaut, incidentally, follows the events and characterization of David Goodis's taut and atmospheric thriller *Down There* remarkably closely throughout, changing very little in terms of action and personality. The changes he does make, however, are in the direction of humanizing Charlie, making him more vulnerable and innocent, and also more comic, than he is in the novel (a process which takes in most of the other characters as well), and the shifts of tone and the bizarre juxtapositions which give the film its unique flavor have no counterpart in the book . . .

. . . Even the gangsters of *Tirez sur le Pianiste* with their jerky, automatonlike movements, their vague sense of better days and lost opportunities, their ineffectual imitation of actions and gestures from faintly-recollected B-movies, and their attempts to impress others with the need to take them seriously, have a humanity which somehow coexists with the fact that they end by killing Lena. (In all these respects they differ markedly from the tough, efficient killers of the book.)

Synopsis and Outline

Edouard Saroyan has been taken away from his rural home so that his skills as a pianist can be developed away from the influence of his two older brothers. After several years he is waiting for a big break while his wife Théresa works as a waitress. One day, seemingly by chance, while Edouard is eating there, he meets Lars Schmeel, an impresario who tells him to come for an audition. The audition is successful and Edouard becomes a famous concert pianist. Meanwhile, Théresa feels that he has become hardened in his success. In despair, she finally tells him that she had slept with Schmeel so that Edouard would have his break. Edouard stalks out of their hotel room, and then rushes back, only to find that Théresa has committed suicide by jumping out of the window.

After this catastrophe Edouard, taking his younger brother Fido with him, leaves his world of success, changes his name to Charlie Kohler, and supports himself and Fido with odd jobs. One day, while cleaning up in a café, he sits down at an old piano and plays a bit. Impressed, the owner hires him to play dance music at night. It is with Charlie playing the piano in the café that the film opens.

Meanwhile, Charlie's brother Chico is being chased by two fellow crooks who want to settle a disagreement about the spoils of a recent job they pulled with Charlie's two brothers. Chico runs to the café for Charlie's protection, but Charlie intervenes only to push some boxes in the way of the pursuers. Yet his place of safety has been discovered.

Charlie leaves the café that night with Léna, the waitress. Charlie mentally tries out several approaches to get Léna into his bed, but when he finally turns to try one, she has already disappeared toward her own house.

Back at his apartment Charlie is visited by Clarisse, a prostitute

161

who lives downstairs and helps care for Fido. He makes her leave early in the morning so that Fido doesn't see her.

Next morning Fido goes off to school. The two other gangsters try to grab him as a hostage, but Fido eludes them. Then Charlie goes out and the gangsters, Ernest and Momo, are more successful. They take him into the car and try to persuade him to show them the way to the family farm and his brothers. Plyne, the manager of the bar, has told them where Charlie lives. Léna comes down the street and she too is pulled into the car. After some conversation the car is stopped for speeding and Charlie and Léna make their getaway.

Léna takes Charlie back to her apartment where he sees a poster of himself as Edouard Saroyan, the cue for a flashback sequence that shows Charlie's change from famous concert pianist to obscure café piano player. Charlie and Léna go to bed. Afterwards they talk about the possibility of a future relationship.

Meanwhile Fido returns from school, again avoiding Momo and Ernest. Fido is having lunch with Clarisse when a customer is announced. Clarisse under protest goes downstairs to meet him, and is locked in her room by Ernest and Momo, who finally succeed in kidnapping Fido.

Meanwhile Charlie goes to the café to quit his job. Léna has given him the hope to begin his concert career again.

But an argument with Plyne arises, egged on by Léna, who is outraged that he sold Charlie's address to the gangsters and takes this opportunity to make fun of him for his advances to her. Charlie intervenes to stop Léna from being hit. The barman grabs Charlie, Charlie fumblingly finds a knife on the counter, and they fight in earnest, winding up in the backyard, both exhausted. "There has to be a winner," says the barman, and begins to choke Charlie. The knife falls into Charlie's reach, and he stabs the barman, aiming at his shoulder. But Plyne moves and he is stabbed in the back instead. The women and the two musicians hide the body and take Charlie to the cellar. Léna tells Charlie what has happened to Fido, and they leave to drive toward the farm to try to head Fido and the gangsters off.

At the farm Richard and Chico, the two brothers, finally explain to Charlie the basis of the argument between them and Ernest and

Momo. Charlie stands guard while the others sleep. The next day Léna appears to tell Charlie he's been cleared by the police. At that moment Ernest and Momo appear with Fido, who knocks one down and escapes. A gunfight ensues. Neither Charlie nor Léna participates but Léna is killed by Ernest. Charlie returns to the café, and in the last sequence he is introduced to the waitress replacing Léna. He begins to play his piano again, looking out at the audience and the dancers.

Three Scenes Not in the Final Film

[The following two scenes are taken from the original scenario of *Shoot the Piano Player*. They were never filmed.]

1. *PLACE PIGALLE—Day (4:00 in the afternoon)—(Tilt shot) lens with a variable opening and 150 mm and 300 mm telephoto lenses.*

COMMENTARY AND VOICE: France, the place Pigalle at the end of a winter afternoon. This is the musicians' exchange. They walk in place to keep their feet warm. They're here for the news, to trade tips: someone's looking for a double bass player at the Paradise. Thanks, have some coffee—Waiter, coffee with a lot of cream—Let me have a glass of Beaujolais—A really black espresso.

2. *The same, but on the other side of the place Pigalle, a light tilt shot to the second floor.*

We see *Charlie* who is leaving the sidewalk after shaking a friend's hand. According to what I'm thinking when we shoot this scene, *Fido* may or may not be in it.

3. *The same, PAN with telephoto to give the effect of a traveling shot.*

COMMENTARY: And here's Charlie, who interests us; what separates him from the others? We don't know very much about him: he's a piano player, he's raising his little brother, and he especially doesn't like stories . . .

Finish the sequence *with a CLOSE-UP—FADE TO BLACK.* (Show Fido? . . .)

4. *SHOP EXTERIOR—STREET—*(Night)
   Chico stops in front of a tailor's.
   Posters announce a sale, he goes in.

4, part 2. *SHOP INTERIOR*—(Night)

Chico: I'd like to see your overcoats.

Salesman: Of course, sir . . . Why are you walking around in this weather with only a jacket on?

Chico: Oh, I'm a little careless . . . Look, do you want to sell me an overcoat or not?

Salesman: Of course, sir, what kind do you want?

Chico: Something warm.

The salesman takes an overcoat down and helps Chico on with it. The overcoat is obviously too big.

Chico: Wait a minute. Check out this ratteen. Come on, try it. Have you ever seen quality like that? Come on, try it, try it!

Chico takes it off and hands it, contemptuously, to the salesman.

Salesman: What's wrong with it?

Chico (affronted): It's too small.

Salesman: O.K., try this one then.

Chico tries it; it's the right size and very elegant.

Salesman: It fits you like a glove.

Chico: How much is it?

Salesman: Eighteen thousand francs [about thirty-five dollars]. A great buy. Great, you can trust me. What do you say to that, huh?

Chico: I'm not quite sure; actually I'm afraid.

Salesman: Afraid?

Chico: Yes, I'm afraid of making a mistake.

Salesman: For a beautiful overcoat. It's a beautiful overcoat; it's one of our exclusive models.

Chico: How much did you say?

Salesman: Eighteen thousand, sir, it's nothing. I defy you to find a similar buy anywhere in the area; I even wonder how we can afford it . . .

Chico: You're telling the truth?

Salesman: Of course, sir; I tell you that if you don't buy this coat, you'll regret it for the rest of your life.

Chico: O.K., I'll take it.

He goes toward the door.

Salesman: That'll be eighteen thousand . . . Hey, where are you going?

Chico opens the door and runs away at top speed.

4, part three. *EXTERIOR-STREET—*(Night)*

A *CLOSE-UP* of Chico running. *REAR TRAVELING SHOT* (*PANCINOR*) centering on his feet. He runs into a lamppost and falls down, unconscious, his face covered with blood. Isolating shot of his cigarette on the ground, burning quickly. A foot enters the frame and grinds it out.

5. *The same*

The fellow lifts Chico up, brings him to, and helps him to his feet. They walk together . . .

[The following scene was shot twice and then not included in the final print, like another scene taken from the novel, in which Charlie and Léna go into a department store. In the scene printed below, Charlie and Thérésa are walking home from the restaurant where Thérésa works as a waitress. Schmeel the impresario—called Domann at this stage of the writing—has just made an appointment for Charlie to see him the next day. Fascinatingly enough, Truffaut recently used parts of the following description of Charlie's teacher Zéleny as a description of André Bazin included as the preface to the second volume of Bazin's writings published by the University of California Press: *What Is Cinema?* Vol. Two, Berkeley, 1971.]

38, part two. *STREET-EXTERIOR—*(Night)

Charlie and Thérésa walk side by side.

Charlie speaks very animatedly.

Charlie: You understand, if there hadn't been any Zéleny, I would never have become a piano player. He was the only one who ever helped me. He was a father to me; he didn't only teach me how to play the piano; he taught me how to become a man. He was an extraordinary guy; I owe him everything good that's happened to me; to talk to him was like a Hindu bathing in the Ganges! He was in bad health, but he had fantastic moral health. He borrowed money loudly and lent it quietly. Everything was simple, clear, and

---

* [This is the beginning of the completed film—ED.]

candid with him. When he left his house for a few days, he always looked for a friend he could lend it to, and another friend he could lend his car to . . .

Théresa: He certainly loved you very much . . .

Charlie: He loved everybody, without exception; we always wonder if the world is just or unjust, but I'm sure there are guys like Zéleny who make it better just by believing that life is good and by acting as if it were. He did good for everyone who came near him; you could count on the fingers of one hand the people who acted badly in front of him. In his presence, when he was around, you were so overcome by his purity that it was impossible not to give the best of yourself. His secret was goodness and more goodness. Maybe that's the secret of genius.

Scenario Extract

In the sequence that follows, Charlie and Léna have just entered the café to announce that they are quitting. It is the middle of scene 46 in Truffaut's original scenario. As in the script for The 400 Blows *and many of Truffaut's other films, there are very few technical directions. I have indicated in the footnotes any substantial differences between the scenario and the completed film.*

Plyne, very embarrassed. He begins cleaning the floor, thus turning his back on everyone.

Léna turns to him often, raising her voice.

Mammy: Both together?

Léna: Yes, together, both of us. You want me to draw a picture?

Mammy: Yes, I'm curious. He usually walks by himself.

Léna: Even when he's with someone, he's by himself. (Louder) To make it short, we're here to get our pay. We're taking this opportunity to give notice.

Mammy: That's the last straw. The clients are already a pain in the ass, and now the help's joined in. They've formed a union, even! Did you hear that, Plyne?

Plyne: (with false joviality) Hi Charlie. Where have you been hiding yourself? I was looking for you because I was worried about those two guys who were here last night.

Léna: He was where you wanted him to hide. Since they had his address, and mine too.

Mammy: I don't understand. I'm out of this thing.

Léna: This thing is pretty ugly. Ask your John. After all, you live with this guy.

Mammy: Live, that's saying a lot . . .

Plyne: Shut up, and you too.

Léna: You should shut up. Look, those two guys who were here last night, the "ambassadors," came back here this morning and with a little money got Charlie's address and mine too.

Mammy: (to *Plyne*) Did you give it to them?

Léna: And how!

Plyne: It didn't happen like that; I thought they wanted to sell you a vacuum cleaner.

The argument continues between Léna and Plyne [see still no. 6] but we don't hear it because it's covered by Charlie's off screen monologue that starts at the same time.

Plyne: You aren't all there.

Léna: He's going to really take care of you.

Plyne: Let me say something, Léna. I'm your friend.

Léna: Do I have to hear that?

Plyne: Would I want to cause trouble for you and Charlie?

Léna: Oh, no!

Charlie's Monologue: Obviously, he's acted like a bastard, but all the same I don't think he deserves that. She leads him a hard life. He sees her every night, he desires her, but he knows he can't do anything, nothing at all! Even now that she's dragging him in the mud, he can't take his eyes off her. Poor Plyne, it isn't his lucky day. She exaggerates; how can I make her understand? And what can I say to her? That Plyne isn't as ugly as he looks, that he's a poor guy who'd like to become someone and hasn't been successful? That's his tragedy, but you can't read it to him. You can't do anything for Plyne, or for anybody else. You're really in the soup; nothing has any importance for you. And then afterwards? It doesn't concern you; nothing concerns you. Do me the pleasure of sitting in your rightful place, in front of the piano.

Charlie sits down in front of the piano and begins to play very softly. He follows the scene from there. He sees Léna laugh loudly in Plyne's face. Plyne moves towards her, lifts his hand, and slaps her. Charlie leaves his place and hesitantly comes back to the bar.[1]

Plyne: Take back what you said.

---

[1] This first slapping does not appear in the film, and Charlie does not leave the piano until somewhat later, after Plyne has called Lena a tramp and is about to slap her.

Léna (enraged): Go fuck yourself.

Plyne: Look at these muscles, Léna. I'm not a nobody. Try a little.

Léna: They're made of shit.

Plyne (pleading): "Go fuck yourself. They're made of shit": terrible words in such a pretty mouth.

Léna: Speaking of mouths, shut yours, you fat pig.

Plyne: I'm going to kill you, Léna, as sure as you see me.

Léna: I don't see you,'you're too low.

Plyne: So much the worse for you, tramp.

He lifts his arm. Charlie, who is nearby, stops him.

Plyne: What's the matter, Charlie? You dreaming?

Charlie: Only if you let her alone.

Plyne: Right now I'm not interested in her, but in you.

Exchange of several punches (telephoto) behind the counter. Then Plyne bends down, grabs the leg of a chair, and advances on Charlie. Charlie rushes towards a drawer and takes out a kitchen knife, like a samurai. They meet again at the end of the room, separated by a football table. Several blows later [see still no. 7] Plyne loses the leg of the char and runs out toward the back court.[2]

54. *BACK COURT*—(Night)

Plyne tries to climb a little wall and slides down.

Plyne and Charlie sit down on the ground a few feet apart.[3]

Panting dialogue:

Charlie: Come on, let's forget it. (He throws down the knife.)

Plyne: That's what you want?

Charlie: Let's forget everything.

Plyne: No, we can't. Someone's got to win.

---

[2] In the film Charlie's actions are both less deliberate and more aggressive. We see his hand in close-up reaching behind the bar and happening to get a hold of the knife. At this, Plyne rips the telephone receiver off the wire as a counter-weapon. Charlie knocks the receiver from Plyne's hand. After some feinting with the tabletop football game between them, Plyne runs out the rear exit of the café.

[3] Plyne throws a ladder in Charlie's way and then tries to climb onto a shed. Charlie pulls him back by his feet. They face each other cautiously. Then Charlie lets the knife fall and they sit down. While they talk, the camera also takes notice of some people watching from a neighboring house.

Charlie: Let's say I back down.

Plyne: No, they saw me run away; I have to get back. They have to think . . . they mustn't believe what she said.

Charlie glances at the knife.

Plyne throws himself on Charlie and smothers him with his arms; they both stay immobile.

Plyne: I don't like Léna anymore because she used certain words unworthy of her. If she had a soul, she wouldn't be able to be so vulgar. She's a tramp, she's not a woman because a woman is pure, delicate, fragile. Woman is supreme, woman is magic. For me woman must always be supreme. Charlie, old buddy, let me be familiar, Charlie, old buddy, you're going to die. [see still no. 8]

Charlie manages to get one hand free and feels on the ground; groping, he finds the knife.

Charlie (off-screen voice): Aim at his arm, give him a good jab, he'll let go.

The knife is going to hit Plyne in the arm when he changes position and gets the blade in the back. Charlie, with a swollen look, faints.[4]

Léna and Mammy come out and separate the bodies.

Léna and Mammy pick up Charlie and drag him to the cellar.

Mammy looks around the court and yells at the people who have watched the scene from their windows:

Mammy: It's an accident; go back inside.

[4] The off-screen voice, which enforces the accidental quality of the stabbing, is not present in the film version. The visuals, however, are the same, with Plyne's abrupt movement landing the knife in his back. Later, in the cellar, after he has revived, Charlie tells Léna that he meant only to stick Plyne in the arm.

Filmography

The beginnings of a complete filmography for Truffaut may be found in Graham Petrie's *The Cinema of François Truffaut* (New York: A. S. Barnes & Co., 1970; London: A. Zwemmer Ltd., 1970), although it contains several mistakes and gives little information about production schedules or locations. It should be supplemented by the information given in the *l'Avant Scène* publications of the scripts.

Short Films

Une Visite, 1955
Les Mistons, Les Films du Carrosse, 1958
Histoire d'Eau, Les Films de la Pléiade, 1959 (codirected with Jean-Luc Godard)
Antoine et Colette (an episode in the anthology film *l'Amour a Vingt Ans*), Ulysse-Unitec, 1962

Feature Films

Les Quatre Cent Coups, Les Films du Carrosse/SEDIF, 1959
Tirez sur le Pianiste, Les Films de la Pléiade, 1960
Jules et Jim, Les Films du Carrosse, 1961
La Peau Douce, Les Films du Carrosse/SEDIF, 1964
Fahrenheit 451, Anglo-Enterprise/Vineyard, 1966
La Mariée Était en Noir, Les Films du Carrosse/Artistes Associés/ Dino de Laurentiis Cinematografica, 1968
Baisers Volés, Les Films du Carrosse/Artistes Associés, 1968
La Sirène du Mississippi, Les Films du Carrosse/Artistes Associés/ Produzioni Associate Delphos

172

l'Enfant Sauvage, Les Films du Carrosse/Artistes Associés, 1970

Le Domicile Conjugal, Les Films du Carrosse/Valoria Films/Fida Cinematografica, 1970

Les Deux Anglaises et le Continent, Les Films du Carrosse/Valoria Films/Cintel Paris

(Truffaut is also credited with the codirection of *Tire-au-flanc 62,* directed by Claude de Givray and produced by Les Films du Carrosse.)

Bibliography

CRITICAL ESSAYS WRITTEN BY TRUFFAUT BEFORE 1960

Beginning in 1953, Truffaut contributed many articles and brief reviews to *Cahiers du Cinéma* and *Arts*. A partial list, in chronological order, of the longer and more significant pieces from *Cahiers du Cinéma* follows.

"En avoir plein la vue." Vol. 5, no. 25 (July 1953): 22–23. On cinemascope.

"Du mépris considéré." Vol. 5, no. 28 (November 1953): 51–54. On Billy Wilder's *Stalag 17*.

"Une certaine tendance du cinéma français." Vol. 6, no. 31 (January 1954): 15–28. The original article expounding the *politique des auteurs*.

"Un trousseau de fausses clés." Vol. 7, no. 39 (October 1954): 45–52. On Hitchcock.

"Orvet, mon amour." Vol. 8, no. 47 (May 1955): 57. On Renoir's play *Orvet*.

"Le Derby des Psaumes." Vol. 8, no. 48 (June 1955): 42–45. On Robert Aldrich's *Vera Cruz*.

"Lola au bucher." Vol. 10, no. 55 (January 1956): 28–31. On Max Ophuls' *Lola Montès*.

INTERVIEWS CONDUCTED BY TRUFFAUT BEFORE 1960

As part of his work as a film critic, Truffaut interviewed many directors for *Cahiers du Cinéma*. Many of these are fascinating documents in the history of his own ideas. The interviews are listed below by director in order of publication.

Jacques Becker (conducted with Jacques Rivette). Vol. 6, no. 32 (February 1954): 3–17.

Jean Renoir (conducted with Jacques Rivette). Vol. 6, no. 34 (April 1954): 3–22; no. 35 (May 1954): 14–30.

Roberto Rossellini (conducted with Maurice Scherer). Vol. 7, no. 37 (July 1954): 1–12.

Abel Gance (conducted with Jacques Rivette). Vol. 8, no. 43 (January 1955): 6–17.

Alfred Hitchcock (conducted with Claude Chabrol). Vol. 8, no. 43 (February 1955): 19–31.

Jules Dassin (conducted with Claude Chabrol). Vol. 8, no. 46 (April 1955): 3–13; no. 47 (May 1955): 11–14.

Howard Hawks (conducted with Jacques Becker and Jacques Rivette). Vol. 10, no. 56 (February 1956): 4–17.

Alfred Hitchcock (conducted with Charles Bitsch). Vol. 11, no. 62 (August–September 1956): 1–5.

Robert Aldrich. Vol. 11, no. 64 (November 1956): 2–11.

Max Ophuls (conducted with Jacques Rivette). Vol. 12, no. 72 (June 1957): 7–25.

Jean Renoir (conducted with Jacques Rivette). Vol. 13, no. 78 (Christmas 1957): 11–54. Truffaut also contributes heavily to the Renoir filmography in this issue.

Robert Aldrich. Vol. 14, no. 82 (April 1958): 4–10.

Jacques Tati (conducted with André Bazin). Vol. 14, no. 83 (May 1958): 2–18.

Georges Franju. Vol. 17, no. 101 (November 1959): 1–12.

BOOKS BY TRUFFAUT

Le Cinéma selon Alfred Hitchcock. Paris: Robert Laffont, 1967; (*Hitchcock*) New York: Simon and Schuster, 1967. A long and well-illustrated interview–discussion.

Jean Renoir by André Bazin. Paris: Champ Libre, 1971. Truffaut compiled this book from Bazin's published and unpublished works on Renoir. He himself contributes a brief "présentation."

BOOKS AND ARTICLES THAT DEAL WITH *Shoot the Piano Player*

* Armes, Roy. *French Cinema Since 1946, Volume II: The Personal Style.* Cranbury, N.J.: A. S. Barnes & Co., 1966.
* Baby, Yvonne. "J'ai voulu traiter *Tirez sur le pianiste* à la manière d'un conte de Perrault" (an interview with Truffaut). *Le Monde,* November 24, 1960.
Bordwell, David. "A Man Can Serve Two Masters." *Film Comment,* vol. 7,

* Denotes those works included or excerpted in this volume.

no. 1 (Spring 1971). A judicious look at the influence of Renoir and Hitchcock on Truffaut's films.

* Collet, Jean; Delahaye, Michel; Fieschi, Jean-André; Labarthe, Andre S.; Tavernier, Bertrand. "Entretien avec François Truffaut." *Cahiers du Cinéma,* vol. 23, no. 138 (December 1962): 40–59.

Comolli, Jean-Louis. "Au Coeur des paradoxes." *Cahiers du Cinéma,* no. 190 (May 1967): 18.

————; and Narboni, Jean. "Entretien avec François Truffaut." *Cahiers du Cinéma,* no. 190 (May 1967): 20–30, 69–70.

* Crowther, Bosley. "Scrambled Satire" (review of *Shoot the Piano Player*). *New York Times,* July 24, 1962.

* Cukier, Dan A., and Gryn, Jo. "Entretien avec François Truffaut." *Script,* vol. 5 (April 1962): 5–15.

Fanne, Dominique. *L'Univers de François Truffaut.* Paris: Éditions du Cerf, 1972. The most recent full-length work about Truffaut, with an especially interesting discussion of the importance of the couple and the child as a motif in his films.

Franchi, R. M.; and Marshall, Lewis. "A Conversation with François Truffaut." Second Montreal International Film Festival, August 15, 1961.

* Greenspun, Roger. "Through the Looking Glass." *Moviegoer,* no. 1 (Winter 1964).

Gryn, Jo. "Cinéma, son amour." *Script,* vol. 5 (April 1962): 37–42.

* "Hommage à Truffaut à Annency." *Cinema 1967,* no. 112 (janvier 1967), pp. 30–51. (Short articles and interviews.)

* Houston, Penelope. "Uncommitted Artist?" *Sight and Sound,* vol. 30, no. 2 (Spring 1961): 64–65.

* Kael, Pauline. *Shoot the Piano Player.* In *I Lost It at the Movies.* Boston: Atlantic–Little, Brown and Co., 1965, pp. 189–94.

* Kas, Pierre. "L'Âme du canon." *Cahiers du Cinéma,* no. 115 (January 1961): 44–46.

* Kauffmann, Stanley. Review of *Shoot the Piano Player.* In *A World on Film.* New York: Harper and Row, 1962, pp. 230–32. First published in *New Republic,* July 9, 1962.

Klein, Michael. "The Literary Sophistication of François Truffaut." *Film Comment,* vol. 3, no. 3 (Summer 1965): 24–29.

* Marcorelles, Louis. "An Interview with Albert Finney and Mary Ure." *Sight and Sound,* vol. 30, no. 2 (Spring 1961): 56–61, 102.

* Martin, Marcel. "*Le Pianiste* de Truffaut." *Cinéma 61,* no. 52 (January 1961): 5–7.

* Pearson, Gabriel, and Rhode, Eric. "Cinema of Appearance." *Sight and Sound,* vol. 30, no. 4 (Autumn 1961): 160–68.

* Petrie, Graham. *The Cinema of François Truffaut.* Cranbury, N.J.: A. S. Barnes & Co., 1970.

* Reisz, Karel, and Millar, Gavin. *The Technique of Film Editing,* 2nd revised edition. London: Focal Press Ltd., 1968.

Ronder, Paul. "François Truffaut: An Interview." *Film Quarterly,* vol. 17, no. 1 (Fall 1963): 3–13. A translation of a condensed version of the interview that appeared in *Cahiers du Cinéma,* no. 138 (December 1962), listed above under Jean Collet et al.

* Shatnoff, Judith. "François Truffaut: The Anarchist Imagination." *Film Quarterly,* vol. 16, no. 3 (Spring 1963): 3–11.

* Török, Jean-Paul. "Le Point Sensible." *Positif,* no. 38 (March 1961): 39–47.

Wood, Robin. "Chabrol and Truffaut." *Movie,* no. 17 (Winter 1969–70): 16–24.

Index

179

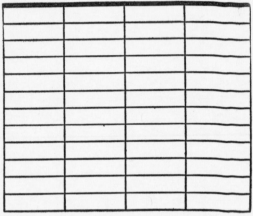